Marketing

Golden Nuggets To
Market Effectively Internet
Marketing, E-Commerce,
Advertising & Web Marketing

Disclaimer Notice:

Bonus

Thanks for making it this far in your education. If you want the real multiplier effect and to take your business skills to the next level, I recommend the easy-to-follow quick tips below. Whether you are running a company or just trying to free up some time so you can spend more time doing the things you love, get more done this week or your money back ;) (it's free!).

Visit https://funnelb.leadpages.co/smarter-not-harder-business/

Top 10 Productivity Tips & Hacks GUARANTEED to Unlock Massive Amounts of Time, Crush Decision Fatigue, and Skyrocket Your Efficiency and Effectiveness

For physical copy, enter in URL:
https://funnelb.leadpages.co/smarter-not-harder-business/

Table of Contents

Introduction

In the past twenty years or so, the world has truly shrunk in size – figuratively. Where once you would have to wait for days and months together to be able to get in touch with someone on the other side of the world, today, it is possible to do so with a few simple clicks of a mouse or a keyboard. Computers and the Internet have brought everybody closer together, giving new meaning to the term 'a global village'.

When it comes to the world of business, the idea of the Internet and technology have made the market even more cutthroat and competitive than it was previously. Earlier, sellers had to compete with other domestic sellers and maybe the one or two really powerful international business owners who could afford to reach out beyond their own borders. With the emergence of e-commerce and internet selling, however, one has to compete with practically the whole world to sell one's products, and while it has made things much more interesting for the customer, it has not been easy on the producers and the business owners.

To be able to capture the market and keep the consumer's attention, every businessman has to upgrade himself to the changing trends in the world. Staying old school may sound romantic in theory, but it is a less than ideal situation when it comes to the practical world. The consumers of today are well informed and expect nothing less than the best; to deliver, the seller has to be on his toes and deliver the goods. Internet commerce, therefore, has become a vital aspect of his work.

Marketing itself has taken on a whole new dimension with the explosion that is the World Wide Web. Where previously you could release advertisements in the newspapers or radio, or perhaps even the television, now you can put up your ads online to capture a much larger market! And the thing is, in many cases, it can prove to be far cheaper than getting a celebrity to endorse your product for thirty seconds on television! Your competitors also have access to the same, fast, e-marketing techniques, so you will have to be vigilant and creative when it comes to putting your products up on the Internet.

If you are looking for some quick tips to get yourself involved in marketing your products online, you have certainly come to the right place! In this book, I have given you some golden nuggets you can follow to set up your own online business and market it effectively over the World Wide Web! Follow these rules and you should find yourself expanding your business very quickly!

Thank you for choosing this book! I hope you find it useful!

Chapter 1 : Setting Up Your Own Website

Before we get into the nitty gritty details of how you can market your product effectively, we need to first understand what e-commerce is and why it's so helpful. In the simplest of terms, e-commerce is the sale of producers and services over the Internet. Your business can be run entirely online, with no real shops or physical space to sell your product. Most business owners, though, tend to supplement their real sales with online sale.

The reason e-commerce is becoming such a big thing is because of the reach it has. You have a global market right there, which you can access with just the click of a button. The Internet has been a game changer in business; you can target people on the other side of the world, without even moving! As long as you are plugged into the social networks and you are up to date with the advancements in technology, you have access to a huge customer base – you just need to learn how to play them!

Remember though, that e-commerce is more than just setting up a website and expecting that people will order your products. It involves as much advertising and marketing as any normal business does, only all of it happens online, in the virtual world. It does not guarantee that you will be able to compete favorably with your competitors – your advertising strategies and marketing techniques are responsible for that! But in the end, having an online portal where you can connect to your customers is definitely an added advantage that will help you firmly establish yourself in the market!

Your customers will have access to you and information about your product at all times, for 24 hours of 365 days, even if your own retail outlet is closed. Adding pictures, video, posting updates, opening blogs and the like will allow you to interact with your consumers on a one-on-one basis that will definitely improve your credibility and your market presence. Your customer can buy from you at any time, from anywhere so long as you are willing to ship to them! In this manner, you can transform your small, local business into an online global portal with access to people and customers of different countries and cultures! It allows room for expansion as wells as diversification in ways that would not have been possible before the World Wide Web!

Without further ado, let us jump right in to Internet marketing and online advertising!

Setting it up

Now, obviously, the first step is to set up your own website. There are many different things to consider, from your payment options to shipment options. To start with, you will need to set up a merchant account, which is basically a specialized bank account that will allow you to accept credit cards.

Once you have that in place, you need to arrange for an established payment gateway provider, which will charge your customers' credit/debit cards through the Internet and credit the funds to your merchant account. There are a number of such companies that operate for this express purpose of serving as the financial bridge between the online buyer and the online seller, like 2checkout.com and authorize.net. The local banks also offer help – they partner with these companies to offer you the best deals. Do your research and pick one that suits you and your business needs.

You can also offer cash payment methods by allowing your customer to transfer funds directly from their bank account to yours. PayPal and Google Wallet are some well-known names you can get help from in these cases. Or if you are shipping locally, you can even access the cash on delivery option, which a lot of customers prefer to use.

Once you have your website set up to all your specifications, you need to come up with a domain name and then get it registered. The domain name is nothing but the name of the website, like amazon.com or eBay.com. There are a number of companies like Network Solutions and Dotster that will help you register your domain name. Pick something easy to remember and add a '.com' to it; then add your trademarks, your logos and your artwork to the site you have set up. Consult your lawyer to make sure you are in accordance with the intellectual property laws.

The last thing to do is to make sure you have a place to host your website. Like any retail outlet, you will need a virtual space on the Internet that belongs to you legally to conduct your business. Either buy your own network server or lease it out, which is a bit cheaper. Check with your budget plan and pick the option, which works for you!

Even as you are setting up and improving your website, you have to remember a couple of things. These are the beginning of your effective marketing strategies and they will get you into shape before you can delve in to hardcore advertising!

- Make sure that your website is easy to use; having a cutting-edge website may sound wonderful in theory, but it will put your customers off if they don't find it user friendly. Keep it simple and accessible and provide your users with easy to understand navigational tools to make their way through your online portal.
- Provide more than just selling options. Don't use your website to simply sell your product; put up information about anything and everything related to it. For instance, if you are running a catering service, you could put out articles on how to plan and host successful parties. Make your website a portal for you to connect to your consumers and interact with them on a personal level so that you gain and retain their loyalty.
- Focus on the layout of your homepage. It is single most important page on your site; your customer's first impression of you is going to be based on this. Develop the homepage in such a way that it is attractive as well as relevant to any search engine

you register with. You can take the help of a professional to set up your homepage as it will remain the most important page on your website.

- Add new content to your homepage regularly. You cannot stay stagnant in the business world; keep your website up to date with the industry and add newer innovations and ideas to excite your customers and retain their loyalty.

- Have feedback forms and other options like an ask-box or a slam-book, where customers can drop a comment or two about your performance or ask you questions about things they don't understand. Again, make it an interactive portal.

- Put up videos and pictures, and maybe even tutorials that concern your product. For instance, if you are selling a computer, you could put up a video that shows how to have it set up at home by themselves without having to ask for help.

- Tell your customers a story when they visit your website. There is nothing more engaging that making your business personal; tell them how you started your venture, what your inspiration is, why a particular product is meaningful, how you hope the customer will feel after buying it, etc, etc. by letting the customer know a few personal things about you, you allow them to make a deeper connection than just that of buyer-seller and thereby build yourself a brand loyalty that would not come otherwise. Also, when you tell a story, you set yourself apart from the other thousands of corporate numbers out there, who simply dole out information and details about their product. This way, the customer feels personally connected to you and will return you again and again.

With that, your online portal is ready and rearing to go! You will need to regularly update your website and build it according to the market demands and trends! Sticking to one model is the sure fire way to lose customers and end up last in the race, so keep yourself up to date and make sure your website works properly! If need be, even hire a web designer who can work wonders with a computer and a mouse.

Chapter 2 : Search Engine Advertising

Now that your website is ready and raring to go, you need start marketing yourself online! The first thing to do is to get your search engine options set up. There are thousands of well-designed websites that offer a variety of different products and services, but the problem is that most of them don't show up on search engines. Ask any customer and they would tell you – they simply use Google or Yahoo or any other search engine to find a product or service they want online!

This means that unless they are searching for your shop online specifically, chances are that they will not come across your portal at all. Most entrepreneurs do not know how to make use of this extremely effective tool when it comes to online advertising.

It is actually very easy – all you have to do is get yourself registered with a search engine so that your domain shows up when a potential customer types out something related to your product into a search engine. It is better to go in for search engines that expect pay; submitting your domain to a free engine will only result in your email address being added to a massive spam list. Going in for paid engines will ensure that your domain gets top priority.

The next thing to monitor is your search engine rankings. If your customer has done a search for certain specific keywords, does that mean your website shows up? Does your domain show in the top 10 results or does it rank lower? Statistics show that then average customer scrolls through 1.8 pages of results before he throws in the towel; if your website ranks lower than that limit, you may be facing a loss. You will have to look into improving your ratings if you want to make your online venture successful.

Managing a search engine is no easy task; you could hire a search engine consultant if you have the money. But if you don't, here are some quick tips you can follow to make sure your search engine options are favorable to the growth of your business. Even if you do, these are brilliant tips to follow when you are doing search advertising, so read through them carefully!

- Make sure your domain name is descriptive; the name itself can be more relevant to the search engine than anything else. It makes it easy for customers to get what they're looking for if your domain name is simple but catchy.
- Submit your name to top engines like Google, Yahoo, MSN, etc. people use these engines much more regularly than others, so read through their guidelines well and use them, even if it ends being slightly costlier than you expected.
- Do online networking; just because you are now going virtual, it doesn't mean you get to stop networking! Networking is the keystone to any successful business, so expand your 'link popularity' by gaining more inbound links to your site. Let other sites know about your site and how they can

link to it, and in turn, provide them with a link of your own or something else they would like.

- Try going in for Pay Per Click Advertising. This is an internet advertising model that is used to direct traffic to websites; it means that you pay another website owner for advertising your link on their web every time that the link gets clicked on.

- Make sure you know the text ad format. All text ads are not created in the same manner; different search engines like Google and Bing have different formats. Understand the rules of each engine and see which would suit you best before you go in for it.

- Include key target words in your advertisement and keep updating these key words. The more the number of key word combinations you can add, the more the number of customers who can reach you.

- Don't include the name of your business in the headline of your advertisement; as such, headlines have very limited character space, so it doesn't make sense. Use it instead, in your optimized URL or your domain name, so that you can use the headline space for more critical content.

- Use proper formatting when you are working out your advertisement for the search engine. Use proper punctuation and do not go crazy with capital letters; these things can put the prospective customer off and ruin your credibility. Also, if you are going to use abbreviations, ensure that they are popular ones and not f your own making; the customer is not going to know that WFW stands for

'We Fix Windows' – that is what you call it, not what the world does.

- Make your website mobile phone friendly; in today's world, even computers and laptops are fast becoming obsolete in the face of the mobile phones and the tablets which are much easier to lug around than their bulkier predecessors. So make sure that your website is user friendly for both options. An even better idea is to put out an online app for your site, making it even easier for clients to have access to you.

- Optimize your website for a local search; remember, even if you can access clients beyond domestic borders, it doesn't mean giving up on those right next to you. Provide a few personal details like local address, local phone numbers and the like so that those customers within your area can get in touch with you easily.

- Claim your Google+ Local Page; this way you can make sure that you show up on Google Maps and in Google's local search results. The Maps are a brilliant way to access customers on the go, and by using Google+, you give your customers information like your phone number, address, timings that you remain open, reviews by other customers, etc.

- Make sure that your website includes some positive reviews you have received. When the search engines retrieve your domain, these reviews will be displayed; studies show that customers prefer to access sellers for whom they have received personal

Marketing

recommendations, even if they have not met the reviewers.

Chapter 3: Other Golden Nuggets of Internet Marketing and Online Advertising

While search engine advertising is the most effective and popular manner of doing Internet marketing, it is not the only way to get yourself established in the virtual world. There are a number of other golden rules you can follow to make your presence felt. Here are a few quick strategies you can employ! For some of these points, I will go into more detail later on in the book, telling you how to use them for the success of your business.

Create Targeted E-mail Lists

Make a list of all your clients and then get their email addresses. Come up with a list of such addresses and start sending them details about your new products, coupons, special offers and discounts, tutorials, etc, etc. the advantage of this method of advertising is that you get to interact directly with your customers, but beware! Lots of sellers tend to misuse this and put the customers off. Nobody really wants to receive a whole lot of unsolicited email that ends up in their spam or junk box in the end.

Go in for opt-in mailing lists; allow your customers to sign up for newsletters and other information instead of thrusting it down their throats. This way, you can be sure that those subscribing to the regular emails are customers who are genuinely interested in receiving them and you have brand loyalty. Also remember, the newsletters must be informative and a little bit creative to keep their attention; you don't want them getting bored and unsubscribing!

And the most important detail – at the end of the email, make sure to specify instructions on how the customer can remove themselves from the email list. This gives them a sense of control and power that can act to your advantage.

Set Up Your Own LinkedIn Profile

Like I mentioned earlier, going virtual does not mean that you no longer have to do any networking. You will have to work even harder; actually, to make sure you have Internet partners and friends to help you promote your product. LinkedIn is a brilliant way to get started; it is a business oriented social networking website that allows you to create connections and do business.

The best thing about LinkedIn is that it is not only for business owners, but for normal people as well! Employers can put out lists of jobs and the qualifications required for candidates, and other users can sign up for those. Businessmen can opt for increasing their contacts to continue to expand their venture and engage others in the industry with whom they want to interact.

In essence, LinkedIn provides you with a platform to access not only your target market, but everybody else from the industry as well! You can keep an eye on your competition, interact with prospective customers and even find yourself new employees to start training. It will increase traffic to your website if only because people want to know more about you, and you will be able to build up a quick and loyal consumer base before you know it!

Make YouTube your Advertising Partner

Doubtless, YouTube is one of the most effective advertisers there are. YouTube videos going viral have been the reason so many people have shot to fame; work the website to your advantage and you will also reach a new height in business! Millions of people access YouTube daily, so if you can get your ad up on YouTube, you can be sure at least a few of them will watch it and be interested, thereby earning you new customers.

Now there are rules and regulations to be followed, of course, and you will have to check with YouTube to see how to get started. This isn't too difficult; you can even simply log into the website and type out 'how to start advertising on YouTube' in their own search engine and you will get a huge number of tutorials and videos that instruct you on how to do it. The problem is making the advertisement itself. Remember, simply posting a video about how the product can be used is not very interesting, and you may not be in the position to get a celebrity to endorse your product.

What you need to do is to make a quick, powerful video in about 15-30 seconds that showcases the best of you and your product. Keep your ad simple and focused; here are a few things that are essential to any YouTube ad –

- Catchy headlines/slogans with researched keywords so that your customer can follow up on the ad in a search engine like Google and access your website
- Clear, concise and powerful message that does not overload your customer with too much information but just manages to capture his attention and keep him interested
- A strong call-to-action letting him know what he can do and how to access you and your company

Remember, you don't need to spend thousands of dollars on professional video cameras and other equipment. A lot of YouTube ads are actually shot with just a small digital camera or even a powerful Smartphone Camera. What the ad in it contains is far more important, so focus on that! Once you have shot the ad, you don't have to spend money on editing software either; there are a number of good editing software that are available online to download for free or for cheap rates. Try using those first, and if they don't suit your needs, then spend money on more professional editing options.

Use Blogging and Other Social Media to your Advantage

Either you can start your own web blog or contact an existing blogger to promote your product. If you are going in for the latter option, make sure that the person you are going into business with is someone who is well established and has a competitive readership; otherwise, it becomes a waste of time, effort and money.

If you can find the right blogger to advertise for you, then you can reach an entirely new set of customers whom you haven't accessed before! A good idea maybe to get the blogger to use your product/service and give their reviews online – that way, it becomes more personal and their good recommendation will work wonders for your credibility.

If you are doing your own blogging, provide links on your website to your blog so that it becomes an open forum for the consumers to engage you. Write quality blog posts that are up to date with the current trends and news items; start discussions with customers that will allow you to get proper feedback from them on where you can improve and how you could diversify or expand.

Apart from simply setting up your own blog, sign up for other social networking sites. Facebook and Twitter, for example, allow you to access a huge number of customers! Use them to promote your products as well as blog posts; engage your customers there so that they feel like a part of something bigger and retain their brand loyalty to you. For instance, tweeting a 'thank you' to a customer, or putting up a status on Facebook about the person who has made the most purchases in the month will make your customers very happy!

You can share business listings from other entrepreneurs on your Twitter or you could post pictures of customers using your products on Instagram (with their express permission). You could even offer to write stories of people who have used your product and found it very useful.

In short, use social networking to connect with your consumers and build brand loyalty. Engage them and talk to them; that way, you will know what they expect from you and you will be able to fulfill those expectations.

Make Use of Reciprocal Links and Reciprocal Banner Advertisements

There are online portals like LinkLeads, which facilitate advertising for business ventures by allowing an exchange of hyperlinks. These portals work on a quid pro quo basis; you will have to allow them to link their products to your own website so that they will extend the same facility to you.

Other than these reciprocal links, you can use companies like 123Banners, which allow free banner advertisement swaps. They work on the same principle; you have to let someone put up banners on your website while they extend the same courtesy to you, thereby allowing for a symbiotic arrangement that benefits both companies.

Use Podcasting

Podcasts are some of the latest and most effective methods of advertising; they are a step up from the radio jingles that were so popular just a little while back. They are basically audio files recorded in a radio talk show format; put up these files on not just your website but other important websites with huge access like Apple's iTunes. These files will allow you access to new age customers who will download them and listen to them, and thereby learn more about you and your product. Make sure that your podcasts are fun to listen to and don't just spew out facts and information about the product – you don't want your customer to fall asleep listening to you! Bringing back the jingle may also be a good idea; it will build brand loyalty like nothing else.

Throw in a Little Something Extra for the Consumer

Free things are the delight of any consumer anywhere! By giving them a little something extra, you let the customer know how much you appreciate them and retain any brand loyalty you have built up. For instance, if you are bookstore owner shipping books to someone, throw in a lovely bookmark for free, maybe with a snarky caption or two to bring a smile to your customer's face! And it would be even better to make it contain a quote from a famous book, or designed by hand to make them feel even more special.

Free trial options also go a long way in engaging your customers, as do prizes for contests. For instance, you can give your 100th customer something special for just being your 100th consumer! Always try to keep your customers happy and engaged so that they know how much you value them and keep returning to you.

Chapter 4 : 13 Ways to Make Your First Sale

Now that I have given you some of the golden nuggets of marketing it's time to finish off by looking at some of the best ways to put it all into practice and make your first sale. Some of these pointers on those made in the previous chapter.

1. Use Facebook to its Full Potential

Facebook is the largest social media site in the world and is also one of the best ways to get your first sale. It's a powerful piece of media if you use it in the right way and it offers up two mechanisms for you to spread the word about your brand:

- Personal profile

- Business profile

The chances are you already have a personal profile but business pages are completely different and must be used in a different way. Let's have a look at how you should use both sides of the Facebook coin to boost your business:

- **Personal Profile**

Your personal page is going to be on of your very best friends while you are starting up your business. However, you do need to show this profile quite a lot of respect otherwise you are quite likely to lose some friends and possibly your account as well.

Now, contrary to what some people say, you can use your personal Facebook page to do a little promoting. However, while your friends and your family will want to know what you are doing, try not to overdo it. Sharing your business products on your personal page has been shown to be highly effective with studies showing that more than 62% of people read this kind of post.

A good rule to stick to is to make sure that your profile is updated every day with a link to a product in your store or to your website. Once a month, post a link to your "About Us" page or your "Story" page from your website. This is a great way of keeping people interested and they want to hear your story so make sure it is a good one. Occasionally, you could share the actual text from the story instead of a link – that way, a lot of the story will show up straight away and, provided your opening is good, it will grab more attention.

It could be that once a day is too much, only you can be the judge of that. Start off at once a day and tone it down if necessary, if you get complaints or friends start leaving you for example.

Lastly, continue using your personal Facebook account for what it is meant for – personal stuff. Continue liking other peoples posts and sharing their articles, etc. Try to keep away from using it as a business outlet because that is what the business page is for.

- **Business Profile**

Facebook Pages is designed as a way of profiling your business and you brand. Facebook refers that you keep your business advertising to your business page, which is why I said that you should not go overboard with your personal page.

With a Facebook Page, the only people who can see your updates are those who have "Liked" the page. By doing this, they have actually given you permission to show adverts to the and this is one of the key points to remember in internet marketing – using permission to market your products and/or services is a more effective method of marketing than the old way of sending out spam to just about everyone. And, using Facebook Pages, you are in the company of the more than 70% of B2C companies that get their customers in this way.

When you promote your business on your Facebook Page, you will do it in exactly the same way as you do your personal page, using links to your website and products, posting news stories, PR mentions, Twitter comments from followers, etc. However, there is a better way to get more quality engagement on Facebook and that is to post updates about things that are NOT related to your product. For example, you could post:

- Industry news and trend

- High quality photos, funny ones, that you are legally allowed to publish

- Stories that are uplifting

- Quotes that offer inspiration

- Surveys or polls that are fun

While these bear no relation to your business, they do help you to form a deeper relationship with your followers. In effect, you are strengthening up your fan base and this will pay out somewhere down the line.

The key here is not to over-promote your brand or your products because people will get fed up. Do make sure that you respond to all comments on your posts, negative and positive ones and keep people talking.

As some of the fans on your business page are likely to be your friends from your personal page, don't post the same content on the same day to both accounts. Keep it fresh and keep it original.

When you first start, your Facebook Page will not have anywhere near as much effect as your personal profile but you mustn't give up. Keep it regularly updated and at some point in the future, your diligence will pay off.

Now that you know the difference between the two accounts, let's look at some things that you can do right now to get the ball rolling:

- Make a list of your friends and family and write down their email addresses to – put it all in a spreadsheet for easy access

- Send each one a personal email or message on Facebook. You don't need to ask them to purchase your service or product, just ask them for some feedback or even if they will write you a testimonial.

- Leave it a few days and then ask each of them to "Like" your Page. Don't send one email to all of them – this looks like spam. Take the time out to send a personal message to each one individually

- Leave it a week or two and then ask each of them to post a message on their own Facebook page about you and what you're doing, not forgetting to tell people where they can buy your service or products.

If you are one of these lucky people, this could just be enough to get your business off and running. In reality though, it is more likely to be a way of introducing yourself and your business to a large audience, getting to know them and letting them get to know you. It will also likely be where your first sale comes from.

Using Facebook for Advertising

This is where the true power of Facebook and your Page will come into play, especially in terms of generating those all-important sales. Facebook advertising has one singular advantage over virtually all of the other advertising channels on the Internet – you can target your ad by specific demographics, such as:

- Interest

- Age

- Gender

- Specific area

Most of the big PP advertising networks cannot do this, pushing Facebook forwards in terms of one of the most powerful forms of direct marketing.

However, before you start running around in excitement and throwing all caution to the wind – not to mention your entire marketing budget – you need to understand that Facebook is primarily a social place, it's where people go to meet up with their friends, not particularly to make purchases.

When you are marketing and advertising, the first thing you must do is consider what the intentions of the target market are in respect of the website that your prospects are currently on. For example, people who use Google are an excellent fit because they are already actively looking for something on Google, making it the right place to grab hold of their attentions.

4 Different Facebook Ads

As the years have passed, Facebook has done a fair bit of experimenting and has released a number of different options for advertising. There are four that have worked the best and are the most commonly used today:

- **Marketplace Ads - t**his is the standard Facebook ad and is the best starting point for many of the smaller and medium businesses.

- **Page Post Ads** - these are the ones that appear on newsfeeds and are commonly called native advertising because the ads blend in to the newsfeed looking like any other status post

- **Sponsored Stories** – These are designed to help potential customers to engage with a brand that friend likes and will only show up in their newsfeed if their friend has engaged recently with the company

- **Promoted Posts** - When you post your update, Facebook doesn't show it to everyone who is on your followers list so, to make sure that every one of your fans sees it, you should use promoted posts. However, while this does offer a boost to the percentage of people who see the post, it will cost you money to do it.

The Right Way to Build Your Facebook Ads

When you use Facebook Ads there is an excellent chance that your product or service will take off like a rocket and the very best thing for you to do is to begin by trying direct sales. This will allow you to become familiar with the advertising platform that Facebook offers.

To help you out, I am going to walk you through the steps that you should consider when you are creating your Facebook advertisements. You don't have to follow them exactly but they will give you a strategic idea of how to think about your customers, how to target them with the right ads to allow you build a better campaign.

- **Determine which product or service you want to sell**

Think about whether you are going to focus on one particular product or service or whether you want customers to be able to choose from a set of categories. You are not limited to one ad and you can target specific ads at specific pages from your website. Don't forget to use the ad to send the customer where you want them to buy the product without having to go through several steps that could put them off.

When you first start out it's probably best to just stick with one product or service, preferably the one that gives you the biggest margin. That way, if you do make mistakes, it won't be too costly and you can learn from them.

- **Decide who the product or service is for**

Think about your target market carefully. Who are they – teens? Women only? Men? Now ask yourself if their location is important. What would their interests be ad what products might they want to look at? Answering these questions for each of the personas you choose can help you in the next step.

- **Choose an image**

You are allowed to put one small image in your Facebook Ad but don't use your brand logo. Try to use a nice clean image that represents the product or service and later on down the line you can begin testing whether your brand logo will work

When you choose your image, go for one that grabs the attention. For example, products that are highly colorful or a category of products that are big sellers tend to do very well, especially for your first avert

- **Write copy that is compelling**

If you have ever created a PPC ad then you will know how to do this. You must create an attention-grabbing headline followed by unique copy that is compelling and makes a reader want to buy. This goes back to step 2 where you considered the market you were targeting. Think about how that market talks about your services or product and think about whether you can write your ad in that style. Remember when you target a particular audience you have to connect with them and that means talking like they do

- **Leave your ad running for a maximum of a couple of weeks.**

Facebook ads tend to have a short lifespan because the same group of people gets to see the same ad all the time. Each time one of your fans logs in, they probably see that ad.

So, be prepared to change your ad every week or two just to keep things fresh and original. Nobody likes seeing the same old ad time and time again and they begin to lose interest. Set yourself reminders to pull an ad, replace it at regular intervals, and record how well, or not as the case may be, the ad did in a spreadsheet. That way you can see what's working and what's not.

If Direct Sales Don't Work...

They won't always work. Don't forget that Facebook is primarily a social place. If you are making a good return on your ads then well done. Double your efforts and create some different ads for different products.

The one power that Facebook ads really have are in that they can generate demand and you can do this in two ways. First, use Facebook Ads just to get a few more "Likes" on your page. The good reason or doing this is that you are able to market to these people for a lot longer than if they weren't part of your fan base. This is because the people who "Like" your page will get to see your updates, not just an ad and that is a much better way of using up your advertising budget.

Second, have these people sign up to a newsletter. As I said earlier, marketing is much more effective when you have permission to market, rather than flooding people's inboxes or Facebook page with unwanted information. Your email list is likely to last a lot longer than any list from a social media website.

There is a trick to building up your email list and that is to find only those people who actually want to hear what you have to say. Don't waste time in trying to get everyone to sign up if only 10% of them are interested; you will simply be wasting good money and time on signing up people who will achieve nothing more than ruining the performance of your email subscription list.

Your newsletter itself must be full of valuable information, something that is going to give your target audience some benefit. Make it compelling, make it something that people really want to read. If you don't really have an angle for your newsletter at this stage then make it simple and get them to "Like" your Facebook page for now. Let's say that you run a kayaking store online. You could have a guide to kayaking so get people to sign up for your email newsletter or "Like" your Facebook page in order to receive the guide. Either way, they will want to see your updates or your email newsletters because they know they will get more tips and information that way

2. Get Networking on LinkedIn

Think of LinkedIn as the professional version of your Facebook profile and you won't go too far wrong. In fact, depending on what type of business you are running, you might just find that you spend just as much time developing a profile on LinkedIn as you do with your Facebook business page.

LinkedIn isn't necessarily about making direct sales. It is more of a business directory, where you get to meet like-minded professionals and expand your network. It's a place for creating opportunities and if you make a sale or two in the process, then it's all good.

If you haven't got a LinkedIn profile already, go ahead and sign up for one now, it's free and takes just a few minutes.

Then you'll need to spend some time on creating the perfect profile.

How to Make LinkedIn Connections

In a similar way to Facebook, LinkedIn is classed as a social network but, rather than "friending" someone, you make a "connection" with them. The more of these connections you have, the bigger the audience that will see you. If you are an ecommerce agent, you need to expand your network as far as you possibly can so, to give you some pointers, these are some of the ways that you can increase the number of connections that you have:

- **Use the "Add Connections" feature on LinkedIn**

When you log into your account, click on "Contacts" and then click on "Add Connections". The feature will go through your email contacts and come up with suggestions of people that you might want to connect with

- **Look through old business cards**

In the course of your life, you have probably amassed a fair collection of business cards. Have a look through them and see if there are any people on there that you can connect to on LinkedIn

- **Add family and friends from Facebook**

It might seem like a waste of time to double up on contacts on two social sites but marketing is all about the number of "touches" before getting the business. If you have a few of your Facebook friends on your LinkedIn connections, your message will become more familiar. And, some of the people who are on Facebook may be more tuned in to business on LinkedIn and more likely to take notice of it there rather than on Facebook.

- **Add new acquaintances to LinkedIn**

During your day-to-day doings, you will more than likely be sending emails or talking to people about your business. If you have a good relationship with them, look to see if they are on LinkedIn and try to make a connection with them. You can also do this with certain customers, but only those that you feel comfortable about. If they can see your certifications, accolades and awards, your credibility increases and their trust in you strengthens.

Don't make connections with people for the fun of it; try to stick to those that you know or have met. First off, LinkedIn doesn't like you adding people that you really don't know and second, your message will not be so effective if you are broadcasting to people that you don't know. Remember, LinkedIn is a professional social site, for professional people.

Completing Your LinkedIn Profile

Treat your LinkedIn profile as an online resume and make sure that you fill out all the details about your past jobs and what you are up to now. Your summary is very important, as it is the one part that everyone will read. Take the time to write something about your new business that is engaging. The following tips will help you to spice things up:

- **Tell a story** – these are more fun than standard resume speaks and humans have evolved to find things easier to remember when told it in the form of a story

- **Be clear about your selling proposition** - it is vital that you clearly communicate to people what makes your business so different, so unique compared to all the others

- **Be clear about how people can help you** - This might sound somewhat self-serving but when it comes to marketing it is perfectly ok to tell people exactly what you are looking for in terms of customers. This has been shown to increase the power that other people have to effectively network with you because they will know exactly who they should pint in your direction and you can do the same for them.

Posting Updates on LinkedIn

LinkedIn differs from Facebook in this respect because updates are professional messages whereas, on Facebook, an update is more about people saying what's on their mind. Facebook updates don't tend to carry as much weight as a LinkedIn update, which will generally be taken more seriously.

Three Things You Absolutely Should Post on LinkedIn

- **Links to the product pages on your website**

As your business is most likely selling something, be it a physical product or a service, go ahead and post links to those products or services. This is business and that is exactly what LinkedIn is all about. Do keep the updates to a minimum though.

- **Valuable content**

LinkedIn is one of the best places to share valuable content that your network is going to like and find useful. This content can be from your own blog or from someone else's website. Take the time to make a collection of good articles, videos and infographics that you can use at some point and keep adding to it.

- **Post your own content**

As you begin to build up a presence online, create a few digital guides that help to educate and inform online visitors. These can be buyers' guides, instructional videos or infographics, all seen as marketing material that can be shared on LinkedIn.

Lastly, when you do post an update on LinkedIn, make sure you add some kind of description as well as including the links to your website. Conversational updates seem to get more engagement than something that is nothing more than a blatant sales pitch or a boring description of a product.

Get Started with LinkedIn Groups

LinkedIn will come up with suggestions for your groups that you may like to join. Have a look through them and join the ones that are truly active. Have a read through what is being posted and join in, add in your opinions while educating people about your business – again, do not use these as places for blatant sales pitches, people don't like it. Take a look at these tips on how to use LinkedIn groups to your advantage:

- **Don't spam**

If you want to stay in a group long enough to make a positive impact, you need to fit in and that means not over promoting your business. As time goes by, that group will refer business your way provide you fit in and join in properly without flooding the group with spam

- **Join in discussions as much as possible**

Take a bit of time out each day joining in with the latest discussion. Show that you know what you are talking about and keep your opinions unbiased.

Depending on which groups you join and the products or services you are selling, you could find yourself digging into a little goldmine of prospective customers – LinkedIn may even be the place where you find your very first customer so treat each group you join with respect.

How to Network on LinkedIn

You know that, when it comes to business, networking is all-important. However, you do need to know how to do it to be effective so her are four tips to help you when you network on LinkedIn:

- **Find the groups that work for you and stay with them**

This is important whether you are networking online or in person. Some groups will work and some just won't give you anything positive. Stick with the ones that do and ditch the ones that don't.

- **Keep meeting the same people**

The more you see someone on a regular basis, the more likely they are to remember you and what you do. It will be your name that comes to mind when an opportunity arises in your niche so, cliché as it may sound; familiarity is everything when it comes to being successful with networking

- **Don't be sporadic**

When you first start out, it will be so tempting to get involved in every group going but this is the one thing you mustn't do. Start with a couple of groups and work your way through gradually, finding the ones that work and staying with them. Not only will this be easier to monitor, it will also help with that familiarity concept as well. As well as that, speak to people who have been networking on a LinkedIn for a long time and ask them that worked for them, which groups were the best ones.

- **Be prepared to spend time doing this**

Networking doesn't take effect immediately but you might be thinking, after a couple of weeks of being hard at it, that it just isn't worth it. You do need to stick at it for several months. People need to get to know you and trust needs to build up. If people contact you, make sure you follow up with them and be consistent in joining in with group discussions.

The most important thing that you need to remember is this – only network with active groups. If the group is new or there is hardly any activity on it, don't waste your time and especially don't waste your time trying to network with people who only comment once every couple of months.

3. Use YouTube to Your Advantage

YouTube is one of the most popular search engines in the world and is an extremely powerful tool. It works well for businesses, providing an unlimited range of creative ways to get traffic to your website and sales for your business

One of the biggest advantages of using YouTube is that any video you make an upload will be included in both the YouTube and Google search results. Each video is a single piece of inbound content that will continue to help sell your products or services for years. And, you can also add YouTube videos to your website to help in communicating the real benefits of your business.

YouTube isn't just a video-sharing platform; it can also act as a form of social network. Due to the way YouTube is designed, it takes almost no effort to share videos on YouTube across various social media platforms such as Twitter and Facebook. This is YouTube's biggest advantage. It forms an interconnecting web between all the social networking sites, thus allowing you to promote your brand across all the sites just by uploading videos. YouTube is considered to be the second most accessed search engine, only beaten by Google. Now that Google has bought over YouTube, it makes it all the more easier for you to promote your business. So, if you plan to market your brand through social media, YouTube might just be the key to your success.

How YouTube Helps You Sell

This comes down to product videos. Let's say that you have an online jewelry store. You could create a video that shows off a unique and eye-catching piece in your store. Your video would show off the design, the material and how it looks, giving people some idea of what to expect. When you have created your video and you upload it, the following three things must be paid attention to:

- **Title** – this is what is going to bring the right customers in so be careful about the title you give your video. Try to use targeted keywords hat potential customers may be using to search

- **Links to your products** - When you right the video description do include links to your product pages. Clicking on those is how the causal viewer becomes a customer

- **Tags** – These are used to attract viewers and are used as keywords to help people locate your videos. Always list the most important tags first in the list.

Setting Up Your YouTube Channel

Customizing your channel is the first step in creating a successful YouTube channel. Your channel is the viewer's guide to your brand. You can modify it to suit your brand. You can choose which videos you want to highlight and which playlists you want your viewers to move to.

You can customize the layout of your channel. You can add themes and colors. You can also choose the tabs that you want displayed. You can choose which video you want in your featured column and if you want it to play automatically when a viewer clicks on your channel. You can use this space to send out your message about your brand and your brand's thinking. If you want to come off as a social brand, then your channel can reflect that thought process and be open to comments. However, if you want to communicate only through your videos, then you can just not allow any comments. If you decide to use comments, you can choose the restrictions you want to place on comments. You have the following four options:

- Every YouTube user can comment
- Friends can automatically comment but others need approval
- Only friends are allowed to comment
- Everyone needs to be approved

The ideal thing to do would be to allow everybody to comment. This way your channel can reach every YouTube user. If you set your option to everybody needs approval, then you could possibly be cutting off a huge target audience from interacting with you. Since you can link your YouTube channel to your email ID, you will get instant updates regarding your channel. So, make sure that you reply promptly to all the comments.

How to Make a YouTube Video

The biggest block has always been a fear of editing videos but today that is so easy that anyone can do it. These are a few of the easiest ways for you to create and edit your videos, with little cost and little experience needed:

- **Use an iPhone**

The iPhone is pretty good for shooting videos and for editing, as well as making it easy to upload straight to YouTube without needing to connect to your PC first. There are lots of apps you can find, some free, some paid, that will help you. Those who have an Android phone can do the same with a wide choice of editing apps.

- **Online Editing**

If you really don't want to download apps or software to do this, you can edit your video in the cloud. YouTube has its own built in editor that helps you to do transitions and write the text.

- **Desktop Editing**

There is plenty of software available, both for Windows PCs and Macs. Some will be free and others will charge a small amount but do your homework first to find the one that works for you.

How to Make Your YouTube Videos Effective

YouTube is no longer a place for viral videos. If you are serious about building a business and promoting it through social media, YouTube is your place. Now, you don't need to get intimidated with the idea of making amazing videos. In the previous section we spoke about how to make a video. In this section we will talk about how to make those videos effective. Beside the content and how the video is shot, there is a lot more happening in a video that you could enhance to make it better for the viewers and to increase your followers. All you need are some editing skills and a catchy structure. You need to make your video good enough to keep your target audience glued to their screens. Here's how you can do just exactly that.

Put the gripping content in the beginning

Research has shown that viewers judge a video within the first 15 seconds. So, make sure that you have your best skills showcased in the very beginning. This also includes the most sensational information. Here are some ways you can keep your viewers interested:

Start with a quick animation. Animation usually catches people's attention. It also shows them that you have superior skills when it comes to making a video. It is the most effective way to build the trust of the viewer. It is particularly useful when you take webcam videos or videos with just one person talking. Having an animated or funny introduction will captivate your audience and add depth to your video.

Spark their curiosity by revealing only a bit of shocking or interesting information in the beginning and slowly building up to the final reveal at the end of the video. This will keep them hooked till the end.

Start with a teaser of the actual video. This is most useful when making how-to videos. You can show them the final result at the very beginning and then go about how to achieve that end result. Being inspirational at the beginning will keep the audience engaged throughout the video.

Use Calls to Action

Every successful marketing campaign on YouTube needs to have a clear call for action. Depending on the message of your video, you can include this call for action from your videos either in the beginning, middle or end. Having a lot prompts can cause a lot of confusion so keep your calls to actions simple. The aim is to make it easy for viewers to perform an action. Here are some important actions to use in your videos:

- **Comment:**
  Encourage your viewers to comment by asking questions or requesting them to suggest a topic for your next video.

- **Subscribe:**
  Give your viewers a valid reason for them to subscribe to you. For example, making new videos every week or making sequel videos so that they can come back next week to see the next part.

- **Video graphics:**
  Add links to your website blog and other social media sites so that the viewers can follow you there for more information and content.

- **Like and share:**
  Ask your viewers to like and share your videos across, not just YouTube but also various social networking platforms. This allows your content to spread across the Internet with minimal effort from your side.

Regular Posting

When you regularly post videos or share them, your channel remains active. This increases your online presence on YouTube and helps build an audience. You should make sure that you post at least a video a week but you need to make sure that the video has some content worth watching. The content you put depends on your goals and your target audience. The best way to have a steady line of videos is to split a long video into a number of shorter ones. Take a theme and build a long video around it. Then, break the video apart at strategic points into shorter videos. This will allow you to post videos regularly for a while till you think of the next topic. And since the videos are in a continuous manner, it will engage your audience enough to make them come back again and again.

Thumbnails

As it is with the title of your video, your thumbnails are a mini marketing platform for your videos and by extension, your brand. If your YouTube channel is more than a month old and hasn't had any black marks against it, then you can upload custom-made thumbnails for all your videos. If you are allowed to upload custom thumbnails, under no circumstance should you ever ignore them. The correct thumbnail would attract a lot of attention on YouTube. You need to decide on your thumbnail while you shoot your video so that you can take the appropriate shots to make a sensational thumbnail. Here some tips on how to choose the perfect thumbnail:

- Take close-ups of faces.
- You should make sure that there is a contrast between the foreground and the background, so that the foreground stands out.
- You should use hi-resolution images. 640x320 is the minimum resolution you should use.
- The thumbnail should look catchy in both large and small sizes.
- Last, but most important, it should accurately depict the content of your video.

Annotations

Annotations are texts that you can place on your video as an overlay. You can layer links, text and hotspots on your videos to add more information to your videos. This also increases the chances of interaction between you and the viewers. Don't overuse annotations since a lot of boxes and links on the video will only annoy the viewers rather than get them interested. Here are some tips on how to use annotations in your videos:

- You can provide the link to your channel and ask them subscribe.
- You can request them to like or comment on the video.

- You can use links to guide them to other videos on your channel or even directly to your channel.
- You can link them to other videos, playlists, collaborating channels, websites and spoofs or bloopers of your videos.
- You can alter your annotations with respect to color, size, time duration, text and link. You can play around with annotations to see which suits your video the best.
- Avoid placing your attentions in the bottom part of the video as YouTube ads could cover them and your annotation goes waste. Embedded player might also obstruct the annotations along the top of the frame.
- Make sure that the annotations do not obstruct or distract the person from the content of the videos. This might be viewed as spam and will actually have a negative effect on your viewers.

The Kind of Content You Can Produce

You can get really creative here. Don't be boring about this and just film your product with a bit of voice over. You don't need a high-end recording studio or video cameras to take a good YouTube video. All you need is some creativity and time. Do be aware that your creative ideas may take too much time though so you need to weigh things up. If you choose to invest a lot of time and energy into making a winning YouTube video, you should aim for this to be your marketing source for the foreseeable future. To cut short on time spent, you can turn old photo shoots into marketable videos by using some basic PowerPoint skills.

Add some music or narration or both and you have a winning video. Don't worry about the quality of the video; just worry about the quality of the content. Regular posting, prompt replies and out-of-the-box videos are what will boost your channel.

Do it right and it will be worth the effort though. Many businesses have been built and fortunes made with videos uploaded on YouTube. Some of the content categories you could consider are:

- **Educational** – you should know a fair bit about your products and the industry surrounding them so think about producing videos like a visual buyer's guide, "how-to" videos or compare and contrast videos.

- **Problem solving** - one of the biggest reasons for searching for a YouTube video is to try to find how to solve a problem. Think about making instructional videos – you can take this one a long way, producing lots of different videos. How-to videos are the most popular videos on YouTube. You can take any topic you are comfortable with and create How-to videos on them. If your computer skills are amazing, then make How-to videos for computer illiterate people. You can then slowly expand into areas that you are not familiar with by using other How-to videos as examples.

- **Video interviews** - especially with professionals in your particular industry. These go down well with viewers as they are getting a professional view on your product or service industry and that goes a long way. Prepare these interviews well in advance. Let your expert prepare some answers to a few questions you think of so that the interview doesn't look bad or sloppy. If you do not have an official channel for your brand yet, remember to keep the interview under 15 minutes because of the time restrictions.

- **Describe fantastic products** - if you have a product that you feel is newsworthy or truly outstanding, create videos that describe them and their features, selling the product by demonstrating what makes it so good.

Besides using original content, you can also use YouTube to curate content. Basically, you can select, organizing and share content posted by other people on YouTube through your website or blog or even on your own YouTube channel. First find the videos that you want to curate. Then, create a playlist with these videos. You can choose which order your videos have to be viewed. You can even use which lists you want available to the public and which to friends only. If you plan to share your curate list on your website or blog, then make sure that you set the privacy to public or else people will not be able to view the videos. To be able to embed the videos on your website, just open the playlist and select the edit My Playlist option and then click on the share tab. This will give you an embed code which you can paste on your website or blog. You can even give your playlist a catchy name so as to grab the attention of the viewers.

Utilizing The Tags

Unless you add a number of tags search engines will show your video only if a person searches for words found in the title. To make sure that your channel pops up often on search engines, you need to add a lot of relevant tags to your video. The more tags you add, the more chances of a larger group of people discovering the video on YouTube. You should also properly tag your channel and add a good description for your channel. If you want your video to spread across various social media platforms, then it might be a good idea for you to allow embedding in your videos. This will allow people to share your videos across various social media sites.

Collaborations

Collaborations are what will expand your viewership. Join hands with fellow YouTubers to promote your videos and theirs. This is known as cross-promotion. You can appear in each other's videos or maybe you could talk about their work and link their channel and they could do the same for you. It's a give and take policy on YouTube. If share and appreciate a peer's content, they will return the favor to you. From there you form a bond with them. No YouTuber will ever say no to some cross-promotion because it literally has no downsides to it. In order to find partners willing to cross-promote with your channel, you need to first devise a strategy and then approach like-minded channels to discuss the possibility of collaboration. The content of the cross-promotion videos might take more effort and time but however, you are on YouTube to promote your business. So, if you optimize your content and your video editing skills, your target audience will get a lot bigger.

Analytics

You might wonder why you should bother going into the analytics of your channel. The YouTube analytics tool is your source of valuable data that you can use to improve your channel and expand your reach. Let has have a look at the three main aspects of the YouTube analytical tool: watch-time, viewership and traffic source.

Watch-time

YouTube Analytics gives you access to the data related to the viewer watch-time on channel as well as a viewer watch-time per video. While having a large number of views is important, it is equally important for you to know how long those viewers are watching your video. There is no point if a large number of the viewers do not watch your videos more than 30 seconds or a minute. The longer they watch, the more likely they are to keep coming back for your videos. This indicates how good your videos actually are.

Also, YouTube keeps optimizing its search algorithm based on watch-time. So it might be wise for you to keep an eye on this particular analytical tool. When you go through your video watch-time analytics, look at ones that have the longest view duration percentages and watch times. These are your most popular videos. You can use these videos to promote your brand. Add annotations to these videos so that it reaches a wider audience. You can also analyze these videos to see how you should make your future videos to ensure more number of hit videos.

Viewership

YouTube analytical tools give you view counts for your entire channel as well as for individual videos. You can analyze your most viewed days and weeks to figure out the mentality of your viewers. You can look into which certain videos are more popular than the others so that you can build on those videos and ensure a higher chance of promoting your brand. It could be the content of these videos that made them popular or the style of videos. Once you figure out what the defining factor is then you can work on making videos that have a similar defining factor.

Traffic source

The analytical tool, traffic source helps you figure out how viewers arrive at your videos and channel. It shows you the path for each individual video. When you examine the source of your video traffic, you can see which other videos are linked to your profile either through similar tags or content. You can use this to optimize your tags, description and so on. You can also use this to form collaborations with people whose content is similar to yours. The "YouTube other features" allows you to find the traffic source for your annotations. It is best if you analyze your videos a week or two after they were uploaded to find out what caused the interest in the videos.

Power Tips

- **Use free links to your advantage** – link to your website or product in your YouTube description. This helps to direct people to where your product can be purchased and it helps with search engine optimization

- **Use YouTube analytic to track performance -** you can monitor how many views you get, where the traffic is coming from, the demographics of your audience and how well your videos are retaining attention, among other things.

- **Keep introductions short** – Newbies tend to go a little overboard here and start their videos with long and dramatic introductions but there really isn't any need. Display a branded logo in the first couple of seconds and then get right to the point of the video. Your message should begin no longer than 3 seconds after the video starts.

  Keep in mind that attention span for videos is short so keep your videos short, less than two minutes is ideal unless your video is classed as an educational one. If what you want to say needs more than one video, produce two and make sure the first one ends in such a way that people want to see the second one.

- **Take video optimization seriously** – YouTube is the second biggest search engine so discovering your video is key to your promotion. YouTube

Search Engine Optimization (SEO) is very different from the usual SEO you see everywhere. Google also gives more importance to web pages that have YouTube videos embedding in their pages.

- **Don't get too distracted by the overproduction process** – do not make the rookie mistake of spending a lot of your time and effort on production and less on content and the actual video. Moderate quality videos work just as well as high quality ones. The key to being a good YouTube marketer is that you use produce videos with a wide variety of content. In the end, the viewers want something that is more than just a pretty background or face. They want some content that they are interested in. They do not want you to advertise your product nor do they want shallow meaningless videos.

- **Apply an "always on" strategy** – The key to being a successful brand marketer is that you integrate your online YouTube strategies with your offline traditional ones. You should be ready to produce videos that target only a selected audience but an audience that is extremely interested in your channel to the extent of forming a fan base.

- **Apply branding to your videos** - You need to consistently brand your videos, not just in the title but also in the tags, description and the video itself. However, you need to do so intelligently and subtly. The viewer should not be overwhelmed by the amount of branding on your video. You need to brand your videos because YouTube videos are often used outside the channel in video embeds and social networking shares. Be careful about over-branding your videos because that might just drive away a majority of your viewers.

- **Add more content not more channels** – Adding more content is always better than increasing the number of channels. Once you increase the number of channels, you will not be able to focus on each channel with the same intensity. If you do not post good quality content regularly, your target audience will gradually lose interest in your channels and move on to better ones. If you plan to market your brand on YouTube, you cannot afford to let that happen.

4. Get Chatting on Twitter

Twitter is an incredibly powerful tool for helping business owners to grow their online business. It is easy to get traffic to your website or your ecommerce store without having to invest vast amounts of time and money into it and it is also a fantastic way to engage with customers. Before I go into too many details about how to make sales using twitter, let's look at some basic account housekeeping.

Set Up Your Account the Right Way

- **Profile Photo -** Make this your business logo and

remember that, when it comes down to branding, you must be consistent across all online accounts to avoid confusion setting in.

- **Your Bio** – This is the place for your value proposition or tagline. Keep it short and have some fun with it

- **Your Website** - **Use** the bio section to include links to your website

- **Your background** – Use a large piece of artwork with your brand on it or an image that has support and contact information on it. If you have the resources available, create something beautiful and outstanding or, if you have to keep to a budget, keep it simple.

Direct Engagement

Twitter has one very nice feature – a real-time search feature. This feature allows you to "listen in" on anyone's conversation and that can help you to increase sales. Simply type in the name of a business that offers something similar to what you do, pick from the results and see if there is anyone that you can converse with. You can also type in the product you sell. You could approach them with any of the following:

- **Coupon Offers** – offer these to people who have just purchased a similar product to yours. That way, next time they want something like it, they'll think of you

- **Ask them about what they bought** – if they bought from a competitor and it's the same kind of product you sell, ask them about it. Try to find out why they chose your competitor. If it was bought from you, thank them and ask how they are getting on with the product

- **Send product links** – if you spot a conversation where someone is talking about an interest in a product, send them links to what you sell

When you post your tweets, try to include a hashtag that has the product brand name. This lets people who search hashtags find you much easier.

Try to keep direct engagement down to a couple of times per day. If you go overboard, it can be seen as spam and Twitter may actually remove your account. Whatever you do, don't send product links to every single person who mentions a product of yours because that is considered to be a gross misuse of the platform.

Listen and Talk

This advice really goes for any platform that you use for business marketing. Always listen to what people are saying about your brand and respond in the right way to build up loyalty. However, if you are new to the business world there is a pretty good chance that nobody is actually talking about you just yet so you need to listen differently.

Use Twitter to show people that you are an authority on your brand and do your best to help them. You can do that by:

- **Solving problems** – listen in on conversations people are having about problems that you can lend a hand with. Think about keywords people would use to indicate they are having a problem and search for them. By helping out, you are building up a band of followers that are active within the industry and this makes them potential customers for the future

- **Talks about the state of the industry** - join in with industry specific conversations and talk about what's going on. By doing this, you can establish yourself as an authority and this opens lots of doors, particular as a business that is happy to accept referrals

- **Show good brands** – if you sell more than one brand, show off the ones you like and use the @ and # characters as a way of mentioning the brand. Not only are you strengthening up your own association with the brand, you are telling people that you sell them too.

Sharing Content

One of the most powerful marketing tips I can give you is to share valuable information. Base your tweets on your niche and share articles, videos and pictures that your audience will like. This will help you to start up conversations with other Twitter users who have the same interests and are looking for what your store is offering.

Throw in the odd tweet that talks about some of your best offers and add links to the product page as well as using that all-import brand or keyword hashtag. Lastly, don't forget to give out some coupon codes occasionally as they may be picked up and spread – that can take your name a long way.

How to Behave On Twitter

Like any social media site, Twitter has a few rules of thumb. First of all, don't over-promote your own business. Think of Twitter and Facebook as being something akin to an online party. You wouldn't interrupt a conversation with an advert for your business at a physical party, so don't do it online. Build up to it gradually and let the conversation unfold around you. As you begin to build up a following, you will get the benefits first-hand. It has already been shown that a follower is 72% more likely to buy from you than from somewhere else.

Promote your Tweets and Use Twitter Ads

Following on from that, you obviously want as many followers as possible but you also want the right ones. This can be something of an onerous task and it can take up years to build the right following. Luckily, you can short circuit things to a certain extent by paying to promote your tweets and you can make use of the advertising feature. This will put you in front of a much larger audience. In a similar way to Facebook, you can target users by gender, geography, interest etc. but Twitter has one big advantage you can also target by keyword both in the search results and in the timeline.

57

Twitter offers a unique model – cost-per-action. In this, you only pay when a user follows a promoted tweet or when they add it to their favorites, retweet it, reply to it or click a link in the tweet.

You can choose from three different advertising promotions:

- **Promoted accounts** - Twitter suggests accounts for users to follow. To get on this list you can pay to be a promoted account

- **Promoted tweets** - you can also get tweets put on user timelines by paying for this particular option

- **Promoted trends** - Twitter lists out the top trends in their user's interest domain and geographical area. You can pay to have your brand name in this list but it can be somewhat pricier than the other two options.

Probably the most useful are the promoted tweets, especially if you are a smaller business Tweets are flexible in how you can use them to gain engagement, create curiosity and excitement and leading to customers landing on your website. If you choose to go down the route of paying to promote your Tweet, use these tactics to your advantage:

- **Ask a Question** – This is perfect for doing a little market research, for starting a conversational and for getting your brand out to potential followers. Think about questions that are fun and engaging, ones that target your niche area perfectly. You are aiming to pick up new followers that will potentially convert to customers.

- **Tweet Coupon Codes for Demanded Products** - If you have a supply of a product that is in high demand but hard to get, you can use a sponsored Tweet to advertise a coupon code. That way, you will get a lot more attention to your store as you are able to get your message out to a wider audience. As well as increasing your numbers of followers, you can get involved in public conversations about your brand and your store, thus building up relationships with future customers.

- **Promote a contest** – Think about a clever contest idea and then use twitter to advertise it. You will be able to reach more people and you will only play when a user takes an action on your tweet.

Reserve Time for Managing Your Account

With all of the above, to think about, it is important that you put time aside to manage your account, to respond to mentions, tweets and messages quickly. Instant responses are much more likely to see results from twitter advertising so ether set time aside or think about hiring a social media manager.

5. Inspire with Pinterest

Pinterest is a very powerful tool in social media marketing but tends to get forgotten bout. It is a visual marketing method and is a fantastic place for your photos to boost your business profile. However, you do need to be a little creative for this to work although the effort is truly worth it. Think about this – visitors that are f=referred to your website via Pinterest are 10% more likely to buy from you.

Add the Pinterest Button to Your Website

This is the easiest way to get traffic and promote brand awareness – just let the customers do it for you. If you add the Pinterest button to your product pages, visitors can pin them to their own accounts and this is a great endorsement for you, especially as it is outside endorsement.

Create a Personal and a Business Account

This is very important. As a company owner, your social network followers will be interested in your pins and having both accounts means that you can double up on activity, pushing your message much further afield. You will find that each account has its own limitations and, as such, you can take advantage and use both to promote brand awareness - what one account won't let you do the other one will.

Create "Smart" Boards

When you pin an image to your account, you can assign it to a specific board. Try to create boards that are focused on a theme, for example, if you are running an online kayaking shop; create a few boards, each one around a specific area that relates to kayaking.

When you assign your boards specific themes, you attract quite a bit more notice. To give you a few ideas and, of course, this does depend on what your business sell, here are a few ideas for themed boards:

- Ideas for holiday gifts – thanksgiving, Halloween, Christmas, Valentines, etc.

- Back to school

- Themed vacations

- Clothing themes

- Gifts for him/her

When your popularity rises, you will be able to let customers add to your boards.

Add Prices to Some Pinned Images

In specific, those items that you always have in stock. Adding a price is simple – in your pin description just add the appropriate currency sign and the price. Do not add prices to items that are not always in stock as this can lead to disappointment when people want to buy them and they can't.

Your Strategy is to Inspire Others

Pinterest's power lies in the way it is able to get people to discover things they may not have discovered otherwise. So, instead of filling up your boards purely with images of your products, use them to inspire others with your products. If you sell clothing for example, present a few pictures of clothing put together in specific ensembles or in specific places.

Other Things You Can Do with Pinterest

- **Create a board specifically for testimonials -** if you get testimonials that are handwritten, take a picture and pin them to a board dedicated tot testimonials

- **Use hashtags -** these are not limited to Twitter! Use hashtags for specific subjects, to broaden your visibility and make it easier for people to find you

- **Hold a contest -** promote a contest where people can create their own boards about your product or brand Make sure the prize is enough to tempt people into joining in and you will have yourself a fantastic form of advertising.

No doubt there are thousands more ways that you can us Pinterest to generate some sales and the best way to find out is to dive in and start pinning.

6. Get Visual on Instagram

Instagram is another of the visual forms of social media marketing and is extremely popular. Much of that is because it is basically Facebook without the chatter – it's all about the photos and it is one of the fastest growing communities online. Instagram has huge potential for coercing that first sale for your business and here's how to do it.

Show off Your Photos

The whole point of Instagram is showcase photographs that are going to generate huge interest and a positive reaction. Do not spend hours uploading hundreds of boring black and white images of your products with the intention of generating a ton of traffic – it wont work. Nobody is going to follow you and nobody will comment – not positively anyway. Be creative, be bold and be unique if you want to be noticed.

Know How to Use Hashtags

This is one of the key areas to getting more exposures with Instagram and is a fantastic way to gain visibility across the entire globe. Don't just pick specific hashtag terms though; use a few broader ones as well. Pick between five and 10 hashtags that are appropriate to your business and you will notice an increase in popularity very quickly.

Tips on Photos

You are not allowed to link to your store through Instagram with individual posts so make sure that you link to it in your bio. Because of this, you need to be a little clever about how to get noticed and how to let people know exactly what you do. You could have your photos watermarked with your domain name but be aware that Instagram crops images to square – if you are going to watermark your images, don't put it in the corners because it will disappear. You could also consider adding coupon codes to your images.

Frequency

Be aware of how often you post. The tendency with newbies is to post loads of pictures in on go and, while this might be fine for a personal account, it isn't for a business page. Try to post no more than three or four times per day to start with and gauge the reaction before you go any further. Keep track of your followers, how many you have and if people start to leave you, it's a hint that you are posting too much so tone it down a little.

Run a Contest

Instagram is a great way of getting a little buzz going about your brand and it's also a great way to get your first sale in the bag. Think about running a contest to boost things up a bit. It's simple to do:

- Choose a prize, something that will entice people into joining the competition

- Pick an appropriate completion hashtag

- Create a theme for the contest – try and have it around your brand if you an

- Get all the photos together and display them online

Provided your incentive is good enough, this is a great way to get people to spread the word about your business.

The secret to success with Instagram is creating something that is engaging, fun, eye-catching and entertaining. Mediocre content doesn't get you anywhere and you won't grab any attention, let alone any sales from potential customers.

Attract Traffic to the Main Content

You are totally missing the point if you are unable to draw traffic to the profile content on Instagram. People often go overboard with adding several links to their photographs, which can be useful to a certain extent. However, those links to your photographs serve no purpose if they don't contain what you want to market. What you can do is, create a link below the biography section of your Instagram, so the viewers can have a quick access. One of the most important things in order to draw more attention to the desired marketing content is to provide links right on the profile page so it grabs attention.

Considering the high number of Instagram users across the globe, it is bound to create more traffic to the content you are trying to market. People of all age groups tend to use Instagram more than the other social media sites like Facebook or twitter. The more engaging posts you share, the more traffic it will gather.

Make use of sponsored content

One of the top most strategies to gaining a large amount of audience is to share posts that are sponsored by companies. This is the fastest and the most inexpensive method of promoting your content on Instagram. You may find tones of Instagram accounts that are created with the sole purpose of promoting a wide array of niches. This includes fashion, automobiles, food, health and many more. For starters, you need to target and follow accounts that are beneficial to you. This will have Instagram suggesting your similar accounts, which may or may not have sponsored posts. The best way to find out if such accounts accept sponsored posts is to check if it mentions an email ID on the profile page. Once you find an email ID, you can send an email requesting for their post pricing so you can promote your company.

If you happen to get a good deal, be sure to check all the posts on the account to pick the more engaging ones that can be shared. An effective strategy is to link these posts to your own Instagram account so the users will be directed straight to your company's website. This can instantly help you rope in several followers in very little time.

Use engaging Graphic Images

Along with the photographs, using some interesting graphic images can increase traffic to your content. It could be a catchy phrase with an inspiring background image or a personally designed logo. Remember to always caption the picture and add hashtags for it to transform into a compelling post. While choosing a graphic image, ensure that it's not too over the top and use subtle colors. Use a sharp border for the image and keep it stylish.

Partner up with a noble cause that is in sync with your company's values

Partnering up with a non-profit organization that supports your strategies can prove to be immensely helpful in attracting trusted followers. There are thousands of companies promoting their values albeit aggressively to attract a large number of followers. When you partner up with a good cause, such as a brand that promotes nutritional diet for under privileged children or encourages people to buy organic products, can create a unique image of your company.

Add engaging video clips

Instagram not only allows pictures to be shared but also permits you to upload videos too. Use videos that aren't too lengthy, yet manages to grab attention. You can add subtitles to the videos to add a global appeal to it.

Instagram videos allow you just about 15 seconds of timeframe wherein it lets you add filters too. Uploading some catchy videos can open a can of opportunities for your company in the social media. Below are some of the videos that you can include on your profile page.

- Do it yourself videos

- A glimpse of making of a company event

- The different products your brand promotes

- New product launches

- How to use company apps

Other strategies to make the videos more interesting:
Use humor

People are invariably looking to break free from their hectic day schedule. For this purpose, adding some fun videos to your profile can gather more followers. Providing some entertainment for your followers keeps them coming back to your website. A brand with a unique sense of humor can garner more attention than the rest of them.

Give out a glimpse of your brand

Giving a sneak peek into the new product launches or creative events organized by the company can make your profile even more interesting. Considering the cutthroat competition of today's world, merely a press release for your new product won't do any good. Social media can provide you a better platform to market your newly launched products. You can create an air or curiosity amongst the followers by managing to give a glimpse of your about-to-be launched product without divulging much detail. Keep them short enough to keep the attention of the viewers.

Share videos that highlight a cause

Remember that Julia Roberts video about nature that recently took the Internet by storm? How did it become such a rage in such a short time? For starters, it highlighted one of the most disturbing causes of concern for mother earth that is "global warming". The video went viral within hours of it being uploaded. Pick the right cause or team up with an NGO that promotes the betterment of society through their non-profit programs. Highlight those in your videos. Add a heartfelt narration wherever needed, so it strikes a chord with the audience. Remember, we are not using it as a manipulative tactic but rather displaying our company's willingness to be associated with noble causes.

Use vibrant colors & animation

Since Instagram doesn't allow you more than 15 seconds for your videos, ensure to keep the videos colorful. This certainly doesn't mean that you go overboard with flashy colors, but be sure to keep it pleasant on the eyes. Similarly, using animation can give a soft and fun look to your videos. There are so many people who would pay more attention to the video simply because it's animated. That explains our fascination with cartoon that happens to strike a chord with us instantly.

Prepare a montage

It doesn't always have to be a clip; you can also create a montage of your company's events or products and upload them in the form of a video. Alternatively, you can also upload montages without sound. There is no auto-play sound when you are watching Instagram videos. You can turn up the volume manually after the video starts. This feature is being added so people can easily access the videos in the midst of company meetings or classes without having disturbing anyone. To cater to such audience, you can upload a video or a montage without sound. Just ensure to add the right captions or taglines where ever necessary.

Keep it catchy at the start

Thousands and thousands of users keep flipping between videos on various sites. Their attention span is so limited that they may just pause the video on your Instagram account if they don't find anything interesting in the first couple of seconds. For this reason, start your videos with a bang, something that can keep the viewer interested.

Capture special Occasions

Be it the major holidays such as Christmas or Independence Day or a local event, be sure to capture these moments and upload them in your videos. Events like a football world cup or elections can also be used to make videos that reach a larger set of audience.

Remain apolitical

Avoid the temptation of including any sort of political topics in your videos. You don't want to draw attention to your company for all the wrong reasons. That being said, don't be too afraid to pick controversial topics. The trick is to avoid taking any aggressive stands about those topics while supporting a particular cause for the right reasons. Making callous remarks about something in your videos can draw a lot of flak from the user. This in turn can discourage people from visiting your profile page.

Be quick in responding to all user comments

Be active when it comes to replying to the comments made on the photographs or links on your Instagram account. Acknowledge the user by tagging their first or the last name and then reply to their comments. When you address the user by their names while commenting, it only helps create a rapport between them and your brand. Do not let any comment go unnoticed, especially if you find a negative one being written on the links. Address these comments with sincerity and explain their queries immediately.

The concept of comparison-shopping engines has proved to be significantly helpful in optimizing the revenue for a retailer. Through this method, you can display all your products along with images and specifications which can make it easier to buy and sell.

Benefits of Instagram:
Consistent Engagement

Though Facebook and twitter is a great medium for promoting your products, it's not as exciting as Instagram. This is also because Instagram is designed in a way that the profile page itself can provide you with a pretty interesting content. As per a survey, Instagram is known to garner 58 times more followers than Facebook or twitter. Instagram being more visual in concept is able to quickly grab the attention of a viewer unlike the other social media sites.

Personalized Engagement

Instagram certainly helps build more trustworthy relationship with the brand. It can provide you the right platform to make a connect with the audience. Through Instagram, one can easily share what goes on behind the marketing of a product in a more personalized way. When you share such intricate details with the consumer, it is bound to build trust in them about the brand. Behind the scenes images of employees who contribute the most can make your company look genuine. Such a personal rapport with the buyers certainly forms a strong bond.

No cost Advertising

Using Instagram to advertise your brand will not cost you a single penny. Plus, it will help you market your brand in the most effective way and provide a high exposure. Instagram advertising can be used by established brands as well as a start-up to market their products.

7. Comparison Shopping Engines

When you run an online retail store, the most obvious place to market your product to millions of people is the comparison-shopping engines. There are loads of them – Google Shopping, Bing Shopping, Shopzilla, PriceGrabber and Nextag to name just a few. Each of these sites places host to millions of shoppers who are looking to grab a bargain on online products and you want some of those shoppers.

Getting your products listed on these sites can yield quick returns and immediate business. Virtually all of them require that you pay to list your items but they are something you should seriously consider.

How They Work

In general, most of these engines work in the same way — you upload a CSV file to their feed and they include your product in their engine. This is done by using Microsoft Excel or any other spreadsheet and then saving it as CSV file. In the file, you need to have certain information specified:

- Title of the product

- Price

- Description

- Location of the image you want to use

Depending on which one you use, there will be different rules on how your file should be formatted so check out what your chosen one wants. It is simple and it will not take you long to get the hang of it.

As soon as your data has been processed, your products will appear on the engine website in front of a massive audience. Whenever a shopper clicks your product link, you get charged and the shopper is directed to your website to make their purchase — hopefully.

What are you really paying for is window shopping but it is an extremely targeted campaign, one where the customers have already been filtered before they come to you and, because of that, it is one of the best places to put your money into for marketing purposes.

The Pitfalls

Comparison shopping engines have one inherent problem – depending on what your strategy is, they could force you to lower your prices and this pushes you into a world you do not want to go into until you understand the consequences of these three things:

- If you want to be the leader in low prices within your industry, you will find yourself in a hell of a race to get to the bottom – the lowest prices possible. That can hurt your business in a big way because you are cutting off some much needed cash flow

- Your brand will end up being highlighted as "cheap" and that brings you a lot of competitors who are doing the same and that puts you in a position where you are no longer unique and do not stand out from the crowd

- Think about the people who use these engines – they are people hunting for a bargain or two and they are not necessarily the best customers. They are not interested in quality or uniqueness or anything like that; all they are interested in price and as soon as a competitor puts their prices below yours, those customers will disappear as fast as they arrived.

Can You Get Round This?

If you really want to reap the benefits of these shopping engines without going down the route of being "cheap", you have to choose specific products and there are two types:

- A unique product that nobody else has. Put those products into your feed and leave the price as it is because you have no competition to worry about

- A few items that you are happy to cut prices on – just a few! Keep those items rotating so they are always different and you stand a chance of bringing new customers that will stay loyal to your brand

However, you do this, do be careful that you are not branding yourself as a cut-price shop and are not doing yourself down. If you think that this could hurt your business, avoid it like the plague, at least until you are more settled and have a customer base that you can rely on.

Are they worth the time and efforts?

It depends on how you choose to look at it but the immediate answer would be a "Yes." If you are a retailer who strategically uses the comparison-shopping engines, you can stand to benefit a huge amount of profit. You need to be tactful enough to know how to sell your product by grabbing the attention of maximum buyers. Nearly hundreds of thousands of products get sold on comparison-shopping engines each day. These are extremely profitable ventures if used correctly and effectively. Comparison shopping sites help you create a specific image for your brand, thereby leading to a significant increase in sales.

Tips for maximizing your benefits

It may seem like you don't have to put in too much efforts once you start using comparison-shopping engines for marketing your brand. While this is true to some extent, you have to keep working on how to effectively use these engines by changing your strategies from time to time. Using comparison shopping engines need a consistent watch on the market for newer updates. Given below is a list of significant tips that can give you maximum benefits out of a comparison-shopping engine.

Use Keywords

Using the right keywords while building a profile on comparison-shopping engines can attract more shoppers. Just the way you obtain Google search results, the typed keywords will be highlighted in bold, thereby matching the shopper's queries. Doing a quick research on what the shoppers generally look for in terms of brands, price range or quality can help get an exact match for their listings.

Detailed Product specifications

A detailed product specification would increase the likelihood of getting more accurate search results. Consumers are often picky when it comes to the attributes of a particular product. It's also understandable considering a wide array of choices today's' market offers. Precisely describing each aspect of the product will help the shoppers in choosing their desired product. This will eventually lead to a wider exposure and increase in the amounts of sales.

Categorize the products efficiently

Ensure that your products are listed in significant categories. Incorrect listings would confuse the shoppers and discourage them from buying. The merchant categories you chose for your products need to be outlined clearly so as to avoid any sort of confusion amongst the shoppers. The best method would be to create categories and sub categories for your products. For instance, Jackets-Women's jackets Men's jackets- Kid's jackets, Unisex jackets.

Upload high quality Images

In today's times it's almost impossible for a product to sell without the consumer being able to access its images. After all why would someone buy a product they know nothing about. Additionally, images with poor picture quality also deters consumer from buying it. Therefore, always ensure to upload better quality images, preferably on a white a background and with added borders. Use tools that can highlight the best features of your product. Click an image of your product from all possible angles for the consumer to be sure about what they are buying.

Upload images of available stock only

It is very important to upload images of products only that are available with the company right now. Ensure that you are updating the images on daily basis so to avoid further confusion. In case the consumer happens click a product that redirects him to an "out of stock" tab, its only going to disappoint him. You don't want the consumer to lose the momentum. You will be jeopardizing the click cost along with the risk of losing your consumer.

Provide an exact price

Consumers do not want to be misled when it comes to the price of a particular product. If a customer happens to view the price of a particular product and proceeds to pay the amount, only to find out that there are additional taxes, it will only create frustration. Similarly, the retail prices and wholesale price of the products needs to be mentioned separately. For instance, the cost of one T-shirt could be $10 but if someone buys them in a lot of 12 your company could be offering a discount of $20. The discounted price for buying in lots should be specified to make things easier.

Maximize the bids of your product

Products that sell well need to placed at a higher bid and for obvious reasons; you need to decrease the bids placed on the products that don't sell much. Products that are unable to sell well can be a total waste of time and money. Therefore, you need to keep the prices of such products to a bare minimum so you could empty the stock. Alternatively, you can also choose to delete the product from the listing and instead upload the fresh ones. While putting a bid, keep in mind to avoid bidding based on projections. Use a comparison-shopping engine in order to get the correct data that can help you decide a bid.

Difference between Comparison-shopping engines and marketplaces

Though it may seem like there's not much difference between selling your products on marketplaces and comparison-shopping engines, there are certain key differences that are highlighted below.

Wider Scope

Although more and more people seem to be using comparison-shopping engines for shopping, marketplaces have a slightly wider scope in terms of being user-friendlier for the consumers. The consumers who already know what they are looking for in terms of a specific brand or price range, they would prefer using marketplaces to buy. Comparison shopping engines would only be required in case of consumers who are yet to assess the products they are looking for. This could include in terms of the price, quality and brand of the product.

More items on display

Marketplaces usually have a high amount of data that is why they are compelled to deal through websites such as Amazon or eBay. Comparison shopping engines allow consumers to sift through different images or specifications thereby helping them sort out the desired information in seconds. This is because comparison engines display only the relevant filters for the consumers to make their shopping experience easier.

Picks the best out of the market

There is immense competition in the market between websites that are trying to sell their products. Using marketplaces does not give you much idea if there is a better deal around the corner. Comparison-shopping engines on the other hand, will provide you exact details that can help you pick the best product within the best price range. It displays clear product reviews, images, prices, features or warranty if any. Marketplaces can seem to be only concerned with the products they are offering. This doesn't work in the best interest of the consumer. Although marketplaces offer wide range of payment options, comparison-shopping engines do a great job overall in helping the consumer chose the best product off the market.

User Experience

Comparison shopping engines provide a slightly better user experience than marketplaces. This happens mainly due to the specific manner in which the comparison shopping sites operate. They provide clear details on all aspects of the product, which also means that a sale is much more likely to take place once a consumer filters out all his requirements.

Just because the price, color, quantity and quality is so clearly mentioned, consumers would prefer coming back to your website rather than choosing a marketplace. Additionally, consumers are constantly presented with the best pick each time they log in to the comparison shopping engines. This works in the best interest of the consumer, thereby compelling them to keep coming back to the shopping engines.

8. Get On Google Places

This is Google's answer to business directories and even if your business hasn't made any money, you still want to be on Google Places. Some businesses simply don't have the time or the resources to build up a good presence on the Internet and yet they still deserve a way for people to find them. Google's main goal in life is to ensure that people can be found and we do look on the net to find businesses.

There is one rule to being on Google Places and that is you can only have an account if you make physical contact with your customers. So, if you only have an online business and you never meet your customers in person, you can't be on Google Places.

What is Google Places?

Google Places is nothing more than an account that a business can sign up for, free of charge. When you apply, you will need to fill out a form with your business information, including description and contact info. When a person searches Google for a geographical location, Google shows results on a map that match the search query.

Disadvantages of Google Places

There is a disadvantage to using Google Places that you must be fully aware of – spam and lots of it. Spammers across the world have very quickly learned the true power of Google Places and that they can exploit it to bring in a ton of traffic from everywhere.

They do this by making up false addresses across a specific geographic territory, ensuring that they get multiple results when someone searches in their area. Google has done its best to make things difficult for the spammers though so it's best to play by their rules and don't try to pull the wool over their eye – it probably won't work.

How to get on Google Places

Sign into your Google account – if you haven't got one, set one up – it's free. Then go to https://www.google.com/business/placesforbusiness/

Fill out all the details requested and double check to make sure that everything is correct. If needs be, you can copy and paste the information from your own website if you have one just to make sure.

Important Details to be Aware of

While Google is a fantastic place for businesses, you do need to be very careful and be mindful of their rules. Follow these tips and you won't go far wrong:

- Use your real business name – that might sound obvious but some users try to put pertinent keywords into the name field and that will just result in you being banned

- Never use a virtual address or a P.O. Box for your business address

- Only open one Google Places account for your business

It is fine if you are running your business from your home but do be careful – if you don't want people visiting your house for business purposes, you must make sure you hide your residential address.

If you do not actually see people face to face at your address, instead going to their place of business or home, under the "Service Areas and Location Settings" section on your account dashboard, you must tick "Yes, this business serves customers at their locations" and then choose "Do not show my business address on my Maps listing".

You must follow these instructions because it will determine whether or not your business show up. Also take the time out to read through the guidelines that Google has laid out on Google Places, just to make sure you are not about to do something that could get you banned.

Category

This is the most important part. When you begin filling out your details, do not put in any old category. You must first make a list of the three categories that are most important to your business and then put that list in order of priority. Now put the number one category on your list into the category field.

This may not auto-complete as some fields do so do take the time out to find the category that describes your business the best. It is absolutely vital that you get this step right, as it is the determining factor in which customers that will be sent to you via Google.

Finally, Google wants to know if you drive to multiple locations to deliver goods or see customers. They need to know if your business can be conducted on wheels because a check in this box tells them that you are complying with their guidelines. If you run your business from home but do not allow people to visit your home address, you must check this box otherwise Google will deny your application for a Google Places Account.

You will come to a step in the process that requires you to verify your business. The easiest way is by phone but do not do this. Do it by postcard as this tells Google that your business really is a real one and it is at the location that you told them. It is important that Google gets this right and, although the mail verification option takes a little longer, it is the best way.

How to get More Traffic from Google Places

Lastly, I want to give you a few tips on how to optimize your listing on Google places so that traffic comes flooding in. The more traffic you get, the higher the chance you have to convert to paying customers.

- Take plenty of time to fill out your application and make sure it is correct

- Add some photos of your business and video if you have it

- Make sure your descriptions are lengthy and

accurate without waffling

- Encourage customers to write review of your business and leave you some feedback

- Integrate your account with Google+

9. Learn from Web Analytics

The key to keeping your business alive and continuing to grow or dropping dead with no sales is knowing why traffic to your site is or isn't buying. That is where web analytics comes in and it will show you exactly what visitors are doing on your site, how long they have been customers of yours and which pages they are on when they exit your site.

Measuring Traffic

The most common piece of information that you can get from web analytics is how much traffic your website gets, on a daily, weekly, monthly and yearly basis. A lot of site owners use this information to determine if their website is doing well or not but I can be a deceptive point to focus on. This is because it doesn't actually tell you what the average order size is, whether the customers are new or returning, whether the website is increasing your revenue, all important things that you need to know to determine the success of your ecommerce business.

Building up traffic to your website is a simply matter of posting blog content that is compelling and engaging or paying for Google AdWords. But none of that guarantees that you will convert that traffic to paying customers.

That's where you need good website analytics because it can give you a good idea of what is and isn't working in terms of your online business.

Basic Analytics and Stat Software

Virtually all websites have built-in software for website statistics and you can normally get at this via the control panel on your website. The two that you will more commonly see are AWStats and Webalizer. Both of these are very basic packages and will tell you how many visitors you get and the top pages that people enter your website on. They will also give you a bit of basic demographics in terms of geographic location and which websites are the top referrers to your site.

Both of these packages have one big advantage in that they both read the log files of your website. Because of this, every single visit is counted. There are other packages that have a snippet of JavaScript that you have to place on your website but the only visits these count are those from visitors that have JavaScript enabled. That equates to around 95% of the population on the net but it isn't 100% and the numbers won't be wholly accurate. If you want to use one of the JavaScript ones, Google Analytics is the best free one as it has a lot of depth to it and tells you exactly what visitors to your website are doing. It is able to detect:

- Which city your visitors are browsing from

- An unlimited list of the pages that people enter your site to and exit it from

- Average amount of time spent on the site

- How many visitors leave without looking at another page, i.e. they just look at the page they enter the site on

You can pretty much find out where virtually all of your website traffic is coming from and there is also no limit on the list of referral websites, social media sources or search engines that send people your way.

Landing Pages

One of the most useful reports in Google Analytics is the top landing pages, as it's a good way of finding out which pages are the most popular for entry point and how those visitors found the pages. Ask yourself these questions about your top landing pages:

- Are they in the list because Google has ranked your webpage high?

- Is most of your PC traffic being directed to that page?

- Is there another website that is linking to it?

If you want to find the answers to these questions in Google Analytics, open Behavior>Site Content>Landing Pages and then click on the button that says "Secondary Dimension" and then "Source". Once you have this information to hand, you can make other decisions, such as:

- Making improvements to the SEO of the specific pages to create more profit for each order

- Reach out to get other websites to link up to certain pages on your site

- Changing the copy on your site to sell better if the page is not living up to your expectations

Also, make sure that you check your top content just to see which of your pages is getting the most visitors – these might not be your top landing pages

Bounce Rate

This measures the numbers of visitors that arrive on your site only to leave again straight away. If your bounce rate is high, it most likely means that either what you are offering is not what they want or they simply can't find whatever they are looking for. This is one of the trickier metrics to understand for an ecommerce business. A high rate could indicate that there are lots of people who are comparing your prices and then leaving or it could be that you just don't have enough information there for visitors to make an informed decision about purchasing. On the other hand, if you have an inventory that is massive, you can expect a high bounce rate because you are likely to be getting a lot of visits that are referred via search engines.

What you can do is install some live chat software and ask your visitors if they need help with anything while they are on your site. This could give you an idea about why visitors are leaving so quickly.

Advanced Metrics and Customer Tracking

You can also get software packages that do quite a bit more in terms of deeper, more comprehensive analytics aimed at ecommerce businesses. These can help you with:

- Conversion Funnel Analysis – Let's say that your checkout process is your conversion funnel. The analytics can tell you how many customers go into your checkout with an order and how many leave without paying. It can identify which part of the process is causing the most problems, which bit is making people leave before they have completed their order. Once you know this, you can fix the issues and make things easier, with the hopeful result that more people will complete their purchases

- Average value of the orders – you can see at a glance what the average value is and know it varies over time – you want to see that average value going up not down

- Lifetime value – As your business grows and you start to invest in keeping the customers you have, it's useful to calculate the lifetime value of them. What you can find out to do this is how much the average customer spends during the time they are purchasing from you. This sort of metric can give you some idea of how much to spend on advertising and marketing

- Real-time analytics – see how individuals behave on

your site – how do they navigate through it and what actions are they taking. This can help you to see if there are any troublesome areas that need looking into on your site

Spend Quality Time with Your Software

Used properly, web analytics can give you a record of what is happening on your website 24/7. If you take the time out to understand what it all means and how to interpret it, you can work out how to fix things that are wrong and how to grow your business. Don't drive your business blind; know what's going on and keep on top of things; doing so will give you a real chance at translating more visitors into sales.

10. Be Accessible on Mobile Devices

Unless you have spent the last 10 years hiding away from the world, you will know that mobile access to the internet has grown at an unprecedented rate and that rate continue to speed full steam ahead. Unfortunately, many of the earlier websites and ecommerce stores were built with just desktop access in mind ad, if yours falls into that category, you can wave goodbye to a large number of sales.

One of the best ways to gain the edge and to bring in more new customers is to have your website accessible on mobile devices, be that phone or tablet. If you can't make your current website accessible to mobile customers, consider building a new one specifically for access on mobile devices.

Check Your Current Site First

You might be lucky here and find that your current store is already fully optimized for mobile use. To check this out, try to open your website on any mobile smartphone and tablet. Do try it on iOS, Android and Windows mobile devices, as well as any other platforms that may be in use, just to check. With Android, because they have the largest market share and are on the largest range of smartphones, you will need to check out quite a few different ones just to be sure.

Do not just open up your website, you need to go a bit deeper than that to test it out. Do the following tasks on every device you test it on:

- Make a purchase of several items

- Do the same but test out a coupon code

- Look at your contact page and check to see if it sends you a message. Then check that you actually received it

- Look at your product pages – do the images zoom and pop out – only if you have installed pop-out functionality

Check on as many mobile browsers as you possibly can. What you are checking for is that your customers can use your website properly and satisfactorily on their mobile devices so do everything that a customer might do on your site.

How to Make a Mobile Website

If your website doesn't perform too well on mobile devise, there are a couple of things you can do.

First, you could rebuild your website with a responsive design. This is web design that works on all devices, be it a desktop, a tablet or a smartphone. You can hire a web developer to do this for you; they can usually make a few tweaks to your code. Not all websites are coded in a way that makes this possible though.

One thing you do need to look at when you are testing your site is how the forms, buttons and any other element that is interactive works. Sometimes, you can simply optimize these and they will work on all platforms. This is also a good time to make your checkout process easier for everyone – the simpler it is, the more sales you will get. Nobody likes a long drawn out sales process, especially if they are using a mobile device.

Redirect Your Customers

If it isn't possible to build a website that suits all users, you could build a separate website structure that lives in a subdomain. Insert a redirect statement in home page header and anyone who accesses it on a mobile device will automatically be redirected to the mobile version.

What you are doing here is not building a whole new website, where you have to pull in all your images and copy. Instead, you are building a version that is mobile friendly and that can call all the images and copy from your main site to show up on the mobile site. That way, you don't need to keep on top of two separate websites and, whenever you update the inventory or copy on the main site; it is automatically going to show up on the mobile site.

The important thing is, however you do it, you need to make your ecommerce store accessible to mobile users. With more and more people using mobile devices these days, they are likely to make up a large proportion of your sales. If they can't access your site, they will go elsewhere.

11. Get Some Product Reviews

Product reviews can make or break your business and one the best ways to do it is to get product reviews from different websites, not just from customers. This helps to increase the credibility of your brand; the trustworthiness and you get the added benefit of advertising via word of mouth. Here's how to do it:

Create a List

You will need to set aside quite a bit of time here to search through Google and other search engines. You are looking for websites that are suitable for giving you product reviews. There is a high chance that the initial search you do will lead into more searches so be prepared to devote time and energy into doing this.

Run searches in the search engines using terms like these (replace the * with the name of your product):

- * Blog

- * Reviews

Marketing

- Submit my product for review

- * Product review

As the results start to come up, write down the web addresses of all the sites that are possibilities. You can do one of two things here – contact them as soon as you come across them or list them and then spend a few hours contacting all of them later. Don't leave it too long before you make contact though; the quicker you speak to them, the quicker you can work out what the return on your efforts is.

There is one important facet to this – in the course of your searches and your contact, you will build up relationships with bloggers in your niche. These relationships should be nurtured because they can be of great benefit to you for a long time. When you speak to a blogger, be genuine and treat the contact as you would if you were networking at a social event.

To begin with, do not end out long emails that are clearly standard and sent to hundreds of people. Keep it short and keep it conversational. Tell them who you are, what you do and ask if you can send them a sample of your product to try out in return for a review. Or you could keep it even simpler and just ask how you go about getting a product reviewed and see what they come back with.

If the website you are contacting is a busy one, with lots of activity, then keep the email short. They don't have time to read through long missives and are more likely to ignore you.

Some Review Sites

Below are some of the sites that are in the business of reviewing products. This is only a sample; there are many more to choose from and some of these may not even suit the product you are selling.

- makeuseof.com

- newmommymedia.comhttp://newmommymedia.com/

- mylittlereviewcorner.wordpress.comhttp://mylittlereviewcorner.wordpress.com/

- 2wired2tiredhttp://2wired2tired.com/

- mommypr.comhttp://mommypr.com/

- thanksmailcarrier.com http://thanksmailcarrier.com/

- thereviewbroads.com http://thereviewbroads.com/

- daddoes.com http://daddoes.com/

If your product is software or electronic then your best bet is to start with CNET.com.

Put a lot of effort into trying to find suitable blogs that relate to your niche, ones that are not solely in the business of doing reviews and rarely do them. Why? Because the chances are, they won't charge you a dime to do the reviews. Also, review sites are not very popular with the likes of Google so if you pay for your product to be reviewed and get a link, there is a high chance that the search engines may penalize you. And lastly, many of the review sites don't settle on one niche so your audience is not quite so wide or dedicated.

Product Reviews and SEO

There is one factor that has a major influence on where your website ranks on the search engines and that is how many websites link back to yours. If you can get another website or a blogger to review your services or products for you, it's a fantastic way of building those all-important link backs and the single biggest benefit of this is the increase in free traffic your website will get.

There are some things you should keep in mind when you start looking for sites to review your products, to make sure that you get your money's worth in terms of SEO and PR. With most sites, you will be able to talk about how your links look in the review so do ask if you are able to specify the links and the text used. If you can, bear these tips in mind:

- Be careful about the link text you choose. Most people are happy to link back to your site with link text that is just the name of your website. Ask them to change the text on occasion to specific keywords that you are looking to rank. For example, if you want to rank the keywords "cheap widget", that is what the link text should be.

- If you are looking for marketing that is a little more targeted, get the link to go back to your product pages. This s one of the most overlooked and underused practices – not linking back to specific pages. If you have a pink widget for sale, for example, you might have a page on your site all about pink widgets so that is where you should link back to. That helps specific pages to get a higher ranking.

This is something that you need to dedicate quite a bit of time to – a half-hearted effort will get you less than half-hearted results and that will just be a waste of time. If you make a list of people to contact, set aside just 15 minutes per day to contact them – it won't take you long to get through the list.

Use Video Bloggers

Video blogging, or vlogging as its commonly known is fast become the most popular method of blogging and, in your search for places to review your product, you will more than likely come across video reviews. Make a note of the most popular reviewers for the type of product you are selling – just look at the number of people who have viewed it to give you an idea of how much influence they have.

Most video reviewers include their website address, and contact details in the description of the video or they will post it at the end of the video. When you contact them to talk about your product, ask if they are prepared to put a link back to your product page in the video – some will say yes and others won't do it so it is worth asking.

When The Review is published

Make sure that you have adequate stocks and a quick way to replenish those stocks when the review goes public. You don't want to find that you can't fulfill all the new orders that are going to come flooding your way.

12. Pay for Google AdWords

AdWords is the advertising network owned and run by Google. It was set up to let online websites put ads on virtually all of the search pages on Google, on YouTube videos and on partner websites.

To be honest, there isn't another advertising network that will provide you with faster or better results that AdWords and the reason for this is simple – your ad can be placed on page one of a Google search query within 5 minutes of you signing up for an account. Now that is fast.

Your ads can also appear on any website that is using Google AdSense to monetize and that account for quite a large percentage of the online population. The way it works is very easy – you determine which ads you want to be shown on Google's results page, based on particular keyword searches. Whenever one of your ads is clicked on, you get charged for it. The cost of clicking depends on how much you bid and how much others are willing to splash out for that same keyword.

The Basics

To get started with using AdWords, visit adwords.google.com. You will find it all very easy to get started as they give you plenty of help. AdWords ads are very simple but you do need to understand everything that goes into making up your ad and how each part works to help you convert business:

- **Headline** – this is the mot important text you will write in your ad. It is the very first line and, if you have ever seen an AdWords ad, you will see that it is in blue with a hyperlink. Good headlines are what determines whether the searcher clicks on them or not and you will need to send time testing out headlines to see what works and what doesn't in getting more click-through's to your website.

- **Description** – Not as important as the headline but still important nonetheless. The text must be compelling and you will need to test out a few to see what works

- **Display URL** - this is just your web address and it doesn't have to be the same as your **destination URL** - this is link that you use to send traffic to from the ad

All of these are the levers by which you test out what is and isn't working so be prepared to spend the required time adjusting them to get them working properly.

Let's have a look at the best way to use AdWords to make sure your advertising budget turns a decent profit.

Start Small

You don't get any reward when you waste money so before you dive in and pick several hundred keywords and bigger budget than you can afford, step back and think. It is best to start on a small scale with a manageable budget. AdWords is not about jumping in with both feet first; it's about honing your campaign before you scale up. You have to know what is working and what isn't before you increase your spending.

So, begin by picking a couple of your products that you know will sell without too much persuasion needed. Then choose a few keywords and come up a couple of different ads for each product.

- For each product type you sell, make a different ad group. Be as specific as you can. Let's say you sell shovels; make one group for garden shovels and another for snow shovels for example.

- Come up with at least two ads for each group because they need to be pitted against each other. This is a critical point for when you scale up and to improve on your profits later on down the line.

By starting in this way, you will find it much easier to test and mange each of your campaigns. If you go all gung-ho at it and do too many ad groups at once you will end up feeling very overwhelmed and will start making snap, poor decisions.

Choose Smart Keywords

Once you have got the hang of AdWords and you are feeling a little more confident with it, you can start looking at setting up some smart ad groups, ones that may do even better.

Think about your brand name and how popular it is. If it is doing well and it is tied closely to your product name, or even if it is your product name, create an ad group around any keywords that are related to the name. Brand keywords tend to do much better and have higher conversion rates than standard keywords and are likely to provide you with the highest rate of return.

Customer Surveys

Whenever a prospect converts into a paying customer, ask them why they chose you over everyone else. What you are trying to find out is why people choose to trust your business with their money. Over time, you should pick up quite a few answers and you will notice a few recurring ones. Look at the way your customers write their answers and use the language they use in your ad copy and keywords.

There is a good reason for this – the language you use is unique to you and your store and in how you carry out your business. There is a high chance that, using the right language, you can convert high and have far less competition for your keywords.

Local Advertising

Use your geographical location and advertise to people in your local area only. This way, you can tailor an ad to a specific area ad you can also set up AdWords to target the customers that are in a set radius.

To change your geographical settings in AdWords, open Campaigns>Locations and set it to what you want. Do this right and you could end up knocking major competitors out of the way in specific geographical locations.

Competitive Keywords

In every single industry, there are a certain number of keywords that can drive vast amounts of traffic. They also cost a lot to bid on when it comes to using them in your AdWords campaign. Using these keywords usually results in a race to see who comes last and loses the most money.

Unless you have a never-ending budget for advertising and are a real expert at AdWords, think a little smarter to gain your return of investment. Otherwise, all you will do is blow your budget and end up throwing the towel in, which is the worst thing you can do on AdWords.

The biggest problem with starting an AdWords account, and then stopping it only to start again a bit later is that your quality score gets ruined. This is a metric that is given to advertisers by Google; the better the score, the better the rates you get and the position your ads are placed in. Google likes advertisers that stick it out and reward them well for it.

Selling Something Unique and Unknown

If you have a unique product, one that is relatively unknown and revolutionary, you are standing in the best possible marketing spot. Unfortunately, because your product is unknown, it can be very difficult to use AdWords to market it effectively. This is because most people already know what they are looking for and if they have never heard of your product, they won't search for it.

However, that doesn't mean you can't use AdWords successfully. All you need to do is take a different approach

- **Talk to existing customers** - ask what it is about your product they like and whether it solves a problem for them – if it does, ask what it was. The answers you get will help you to write the best ad to bring in new customers.

- **Determine what the benefits of your products are** - in the same way as it does when you talk to your customers, working out the real benefits of your products can help you to construct the right keywords and the right campaigns to show that your product can solve problems that people have.

Another great way to raise some awareness of your product is through content marketing, especially when you don't have an active sales volume to speak for you. Write some great articles and publish them on content directories. Lin to them on your website, in your Facebook and twitter accounts and any other place you can think of.

Track Your Conversions

When you are doing PPC, or Pay-Per-Click advertising, this is one of the most important parts of doing it right. Conversions are when a person clicks your ad, arrives t your store and makes a purchase from you and thee are the single most important metric that will determine which keywords are right to use and what you write in your ad.

Let's go back to the shovels. If you were to track your conversions, you might see that, while "heavy duty shovels" has a high click-through rate, it does not convert as well as "shovel". When you do the number crunching you might find that, instead of making money, you are actually losing on the first keyword, "heavy duty shovels". In this case, you can do a number of things:

- **Be patient** – Wait until sufficient time has gone by before you know for sure that the keyword is losing you money. It's no good looking after a one-day or even one-week, because it just isn't enough time. You need plenty of data to support whatever decision you make

- **Pause that specific keyword** - after a couple of weeks, you will know if the keyword is doing its job. If it isn't, put a pause on it. This stops the ad from showing up when a person runs a search for that particular keyword

- **Come up with a new ad and ad group** – you know in your heart that this is a fantastic item and it should sell like hotcakes. Maybe you just need to refine things a little more so come up with a new ad group and write a new ad for the product. Be more specific in your ad. If you use the product name in your keyword and in the headline, you should get much better results.

You can't possibly make informed decisions or know what the return on your investment is without knowing what the conversion rate of each keyword is. Set up conversion tracking as a matter of importance.

Testing

The real beauty of tracking your conversions is that it gives you free reign to test out new keywords and new ad copy. The goal of any AdWords campaign is to iterate on new keywords and new ads that perform much better than the preceding ones.

Let's say that you have two ads running in one ad group. Both use the same keywords but one ad is performing much better than the other, resulting in much higher conversions. In this case, you would pause the underperforming ad and come up with a new one that will work better than the ad that is already performing high.

Think of it as something akin to a competition between your ads. You want to keep on perfecting it, getting better and getting higher conversion rates and, as a result, more profit. And profit is the name of the AdWords game.

The World at Your Feet

The real beauty of AdWords is that it gives you full and open access to the search audience across the entire globe. It all comes down to how well you construct your campaign and how intelligently you use AdWords.

Start slow and steady and do not throw in the towel. Stick at it, continually test out new keywords and new ads and never forget that, not only are you trying to sell your products, you are trying to gain new lifelong customers

13. Be Persistent

By now, you should have tried lots of different ways, loads of strategies to try to get your first online sale. It is perfectly possible to overdo things; to jump in feet first and try to do too much this can leave you feeling somewhat overwhelmed and overworked, especially when you are not seeing any results for all your effort.

I am going to give you one last piece of advice on how to be successful at managing several different tactics at the same time. This way, you can optimize your time, your budget and your business. The result should be quicker results and more profit:

Test, Measure and Then Repeat

Make sure that you measure the results of any marketing activity very carefully. Think of running a business as being something like a science experiment – one wrong move and it can all blow up in your face. It is so easy to test all the different strategies and tactics that you use and just assume that you will remember whether they worked or not. Always record your results – that way you will never be able to forget them.

Make it a habit to record your results and measuring what you are doing because this is the only way that you can determine how and when to grow your business. The data you collect can give you some strong insights on what you should and should not be doing and what else you could try.

While you may think that this is going to take up too much of your time, remember that this is what business is all about. This is how you can make the right decisions to grow your brand and increase your profit and, eventually, you might just find yourself in the position to be able to hire someone to do all this for you.

- ***Choosing What Works***

When you have taken the time out to record all your results, you will be able to see exactly what is and what isn't working for you. However, instead of picking the top three methods in sales and marketing, for example, you should look at the list and pick out, not just the ones that worked best, but also those that worked naturally.

If a strategy fits in with the way you naturally work, the chances are it is the best one for you. If a strategy causes any friction to your workflow, it isn't the best way to do things.

Double up on the activities that really worked for you and work out how you can make them work even better Ask yourself a few questions:

- Can I streamline this process or even automate some parts of it?

- Can I hire someone to do this for me?

- What can I do to make the whole process easier for me and for my company?

Marketing

Taking on too much in one go will get you on the road to nowhere fast. Keep these things in mind:

- Focus on one thing at a time for the best results.

- Trying to do too much at once will result in mediocre or bad work

- You only have so much energy – use it wisely.

Chapter 5: AdSense and Adwords

When you own a popular blog or website, there are many ways in which you can capitalize upon its potential. It does not always have to deal with increasing the number of customers you have and can also deal with monetizing your popularity.

This means that every time someone visits your page or channel, you have the chance to make money out of it. I'm sure you are aware of affiliate marketing and how it operates-you tie up with companies and host their links on your site. However, it can be a bit of a pain to look for the best companies to tie up with and tougher to incorporate their links on your site. You have to look into each and every detail and make sure that you are subtly promoting them.

But what if there was a way for you to avoid all of the above hassles and have someone else do all the dirty work for you? Wouldn't it be awesome to have someone place the ads for you while you simply kick back and relax? Well, here is how you can do so.

AdSense and adwords are both owned and operated by Google and are software that allows people to make money from their websites.

AdSense is unique software that places ads on your website or YouTube channel based on what your customers are most likely going to be interested in buying.

The software is extremely smart and will base its ads on what your customers are looking at on your site. For example, if your YouTube video is about cleansing teeth, AdSense will play an ad of whitening toothpaste. So, you don't have to do anything for it and the software will do it for you.

Every time your customer clicks on the ad, they will be redirected to the particular company's website. If they purchase what they find there, then part of the sales proceeds will be credited to your account. Sometimes, just clicking on the ad can garner your monetary benefits.

Adwords on the other hand, will start playing ads based on the key words that your viewer is typing into the search box. For example, if he or she types in Christmas gifts then ads pertaining to gift shops will play. Here too, the viewer will be redirected to another site from where the ad will be playing.

There are many options to pick from in terms of where you would like the ad to be placed. You can choose the top half or the bottom half or somewhere on the sides. It is always best to pick the top half of the fold, as the ads will be more visible.

You can also pick the size of the box that will play the ads. There will be choices to pick from and you can choose the one that best fits the dimensions of your site.

There are some rules that you have to follow when you wish to make use of AdSense and adwords. For example, you have to make sure that you don't click on the ads yourself. Google is very smart and will immediately know based on the IP address. The most you can do is get friends and family members to click but those will have to be unique hits.

The signing up process is quite simple and you don't have to fill in too many columns. But ensure that you add in all the right details. You will be paid on the 15th of each month and have to reach a minimum balance for it. Google will transfer the money into the account that you have linked to your account.

There is no upper limit to how much you can make from your ads. Many companies make thousands of dollars a month through their AdSense and adwords accounts alone. You too can do the same provided you sign up at the earliest.

Remember that most ads will give the customer a chance to skip it, which means that they need not sit through the whole thing. This can be a bad thing as you cannot control people's actions and if a majority skips then that can significantly impact your monetization. One-way to prevent this is to request for smaller ads that run fast and don't provide the option of skipping. That way, you can easily prevent people skipping ads; even if they click on the ad by mistake, they will be redirected and you will be credited.

Once you establish yourself, you have to maintain your account and keep adding in new content. You have to capture your viewer's attention and ensure that they are hooked to the content you provide them.

Chapter 6 : Dos and Don'ts of YouTube Channel

Here are the dos and don'ts of YouTube channels.

Dos

<u>Keep posting</u>

It is important for you to keep your YouTube page updated. Don't make the mistake of stopping with the videos just because you have the desired audience already. You have to post to hold on to them as well. The content needs to be unique and help people relate to it. Don't keep giving them what they have already seen. Give them something else for a change and see the impact that it will have on them. You have to maintain records of everything that you post so that you can keep track of people's interests.

<u>Build up networks</u>

You have to build up a network of people that will contribute towards the upkeep of your channel. You have to subscribe to others that you think can influence your business. You have to also reach out to them in order to collaborate with them. You have to remain updated on who is doing well on YouTube and who you should be subscribing to in order to get noticed by many customers.

Collaborate wisely

You have to remember to collaborate wisely. Don't base your decision on the terms of friendship. You have to find someone that is just as popular and influential as you. If you don't, then you will be doing someone a big favor and gaining nothing out of it. If you plan on helping someone with their viewers then you must charge for it whatever fees you think deems fit for your services. When you pick the person to collaborate with, you must check the number of subscribers they have and the over views that their videos have garnered. More is always good, you can ask them to help you increase your numbers and be ready to pay if they are very influential. Remember that collaborations need not always be with others on YouTube and you can also collaborate with people on Instagram or Facebook or a popular blogger.

Edit professionally

When you wish to upload a video on YouTube, you have to ensure that it is professionally edited and has all the elements of a viral video. Treat each one like it is the most important video and make use of tricks that you know will attract a crowd. You must make use of tools that help you achieve a professional look. If you are not adept at it then you can take the help of someone that is good at professionally editing. Once you are done, you can upload the videos and ask for honest opinions. Whether it is a commercial that you have uploaded or a demonstration video, you have to pass it around to get an honest opinion on it. If people have pointed out some changes that need to be made then you must make them to better the video.

Reply to Comments

It is important to reply to any comments that have been posted under the videos. You should try and ignore the bashful ones as they are useless and unnecessary and focus only on the serious comments. Answering them will help you connect with your audience. You can employ someone to do it for you if you are busy. You can also consider employing a group that can reply to multiple comments.

These form the different dos of YouTube.

Don'ts

Don't copy

Do not copy any content from someone else and stick with what you think is best for your channel. If something is trending then maybe you can have a small tribute in between your video but to entirely make it about the other topic might make it seem like you are simply copying. Make it unique in order to create a unique identity for yourself.

Don't forget to revamp

You have to remember to revamp your channel from time to time. Don't make it simple, as your audience will find it boring. Capitalize on shock value and give them something that they were not expecting at all. It need not be something extremely out of the ordinary and can be something that will get them thinking. Make it look different every few months to generate mass interest.

Don't block comments

Many people make the mistake of blocking comments on their channel, which is pretty stupid. In a bid to escape the unnecessary comments, they end up blocking them altogether. Instead, you should block out just the bad comments and focus on the positive ones. With time, you will be able to master the art of contemplating just the best comments and ignoring the rest.

Don't be impatient

It is important to give everything due time to grow and nurture. Don't be in a hurry to see results. If you remain impatient then you won't see the results that you deserve to. By remaining patient, you will be able to attain a bigger view count as well. Set yourself targets every month that you wish to attain and then go after it. That would be a great way to keep track of your views.

Don't forget call to action

It is important to remind people to subscribe or like or visit your website etc. It pays to spoon-feed your audience, as they might not know to do these things by themselves. You must put in efforts to lay it out in front of them for them to take notice of it.

Marketing

These form the different don'ts for your YouTube channel.

Chapter 7: Social Media Exclusives

There are many social media exclusive deals that you can offer to your customers. In this chapter, we will look at some of them in detail.

Offer online discounts

You can offer your customers social media exclusive discounts. These refer to discounts that they will only get on your social media pages and not at the stores. You can inform your customers when they visit your store that they can avail a discount by buying through Facebook or twitter. That is a great way to divert them over. Remember that the discounts have to be sizeable enough for them to take notice. If you offer them something small then it might not appeal to them. 5 or 10% will not cut it; you have to offer them 15 or 20%. Remember that this should be different from any sale that is on. It has to be an added benefit. Or you can offer the discount after the sale period is over.

Offer Exclusives

You can come up with a range of products that people can only buy from your social media sites. These can be exclusive items that they will not get in the store or any other place. You can come up with a range of these so that they can pick what they like from it. Don't offer them something they have already seen before, give them reason to visit your site and choose something nice for themselves. The pricing should be same as the other products that they can buy from stores.

Provide After sales service

You can provide after sales services to them through your social media account. As you know, after sales services are extremely important and you should provide good services to keep your customers happy. One idea is to tell them that they can avail the services only through your social media sites where your customer support team can be reached. You can add in numbers and links to places where they can raise a query or seek solution to an issue with the products they have purchased. Providing after sales services to your customers will help you create return customers, which is extremely important for any business.

Host Tie-ups

You can tie up with other brands and companies as well. Tying up can refer to collaborating and creating unique merchandize that the two of you offer to your customers or can also relate to one offering a discount on the other's products. Say for example you offer a 10% discount on the other company's products if your customers buy yours. Similarly, the other company can issue a coupon code that will help their customers avail your products at a discount. Such tie-ups are a great way to increase your customer base, as you and your collaborator will exchange each other's.

Personalized merchandize

You can offer your customers some personalized merchandize as well. This can be products that carry something unique like the customer's name or a design that they have chosen for themselves etc. Personalizing merchandize will help them connect better with you and you can better equip your knowledge on customers' tastes and habits. You must maintain a record of what they have customized so that you can give them the same next time.

Organize Contests

It is a great idea for you to organize contests. These can be contests asking people to come up with ideas for something or submitting drawings, slogans etc. These contests should be open to only those that have liked your Facebook page or are following you on twitter etc. Organizing contests will also help you know how many actively visit your page and are interested in taking part in such activities. The prizes that you offer to winners should be interesting enough for them to participate in your contests.

Sign up rewards

You have to offer rewards to people when they sign up or subscribe to your social media sites. These can be discount coupons, free samples and other such offers. You must send them emails mentioning these offers and tell them what they will be getting if they sign up with you. You need not run the offer forever, you have to have a target audience in mind and as soon as the target is reached, you can stop the offer. You can then shoot out emails to the others saying how they missed out on an offer but can check back to find others.

Giving feedback

You can encourage people to leave a feedback behind on your social media sites. You can ask them to leave behind a review or rating so that you know what to make for them next. You have to mention it on all your products so that they know where to find you and leave behind a rating.

Events

You can organize events for your customers where they can meet up and discuss your products and services. You don't have to make it a grand affair; you can organize just a small event where you invite your best customers. There, you can ask those questions about the company and products. You can also get them to bring with them someone that they think might be interested in their products.

These form the different social media only offers that you can offer your customers. Remember that this list is not exhaustive and there are many other things that you can do as well. You have to spend some time thinking it up and putting it into practice.

Chapter 8: Organizing Contests and Social Promotion – Instagram and Twitter E-Marketing

Twitter and Instagram are possibly the most powerful social media tools you can use to promote yourself other than Facebook, Pinterest and the like. It goes without saying that you must sync all your social media accounts together so that you can augment one effort with the other. That way, when you conduct a promotional campaign on one account, it gets updated automatically on the other and the customers can view your campaign on all platforms.

That being said, there are certain tips you should keep in mind when you conduct marketing campaigns on Instagram and Twitter. Contests are best hosted on these two platforms; Facebook can also be used, but the limited space and characters that these offer end up being a nice tease that will rouse the customer's curiosity in a way that Facebook cannot. Before we get into contest organization, however, check out these marketing options that they have to offer.

Over the years that Instagram has been functioning, a lot of small businesses have used it to promote their business ventures. It became such a popular idea that the owners decided to make a service itself – a blog named Instagram for Business was started, which offers small business owners marketing strategy ideas to gain visibility for their ventures. The blog also serves as a platform for you to make contact with other business who use Instagram to market; there are guidelines available on what advertisements are best suited to Instagram, how to partner up with other businessmen on Instagram, etc.

You can also try to use the sponsored ads on Instagram. As the name suggests, these are the ads that you pay for; there are sponsored ad accounts that are set up precisely for the purpose of giving shout-outs to those businessmen who are willing to pay for it. The advantage of this type of advertising is that it's cheaper than making an ad of your own – and these accounts reach a large number of people who Follow them, so you can reach out to a wide audience.

On Twitter, other than contests, there are three major types of campaigns that you can conduct to promote your business. The first is the 'Twixclusive', which is something that has been gaining fast popularity among business owners in the past few years. As you can probably guess, 'Twixclusive' is a mash up of the words 'Twitter' and 'Exclusive'. Obviously, it means that you put something special only on Twitter and any interested, prospective customers must follow you there to get a glimpse of it.

This something special is generally an offer or a discount that is available only on Twitter. Your followers feel like they are in on a special secret and they will retweet as much as they can, making you a trending topic and helping you gain more visibility. Here are the three most popular 'Twixclusives' that businesses use to promote -

- Special Offers and Limited-Time Discounts – Put up an offer on Twitter that has a limited time period; keep your offer catchy, simple and easy to understand and then provide a link to your website where they can avail of the offer using the unique coupon code. Make sure your hashtag 'Twixclusive', since that's what most customers will be searching for.
- Videos and Photos – These need not necessarily sell a product; they are simply a way to engage your audience and build further brand loyalty. Post pictures, videos and images that give your customers a taste of what happens behind the scenes. Tweet about the upcoming 'Twixclusive' and then on allotted day, engage your customers by tweeting pictures, videos as well talking to them directly.
- Q&As – Bloggers and Vloggers will know; these are the best way to get your audience involved. Invite your audience to ask you questions directly on a 'Twixclusive' and then answer them; again, you're not really selling a product, but you are building brand loyalty, which is extremely important! Your followers will special, feel like they've been let in on a secret and they will become return customers and spread word about you.

As you can see, some of these require real time, live conversations taking place. This leads me to the second type of Twitter Marketing you can do – LiveTweeting. This is actually a very popular promotion method that is used all too often on Twitter – by celebrities. You've probably come across a number of famous actors throwing out LiveTweet when the new episode of their show comes out. It's a great way to keep the audience riveted and engaged and it brings about wonderful visibility for their shows.

The concept can apply to you as a small business owner as well, though the process is a lot trickier. Given that you're definitely not as popular as a celebrity, you need to be smarter about it. A good idea is to combine LiveTweeting with a Twixclusive – provide a Q&A Session or a Video-Posting of a Team Building Exercise within your company; on the assigned date, have a LiveTweet session with your audience about the process itself and how you and your team felt. Give them the insider scoop and make them feel like part of the family – your brand loyalty will soar to new heights.

The third type of Twitter campaign that you can run is the Flock to Unflock Campaign, which has also been gaining a lot of popularity over the years. What you are essentially doing is getting your Twitter followers to do your promotion for you; the premise of the campaign is that your followers retweet your promotional tweet a specified number of times to unlock exclusive content from you. This content could be anything – an offer, a video, a discount, a free sample – anything that serves as an incentive for them to consistently retweet your promotional tweet. Here are the simple steps involved in a Flock to Unflock Campaign –

- Figure out an incentive that your followers would like. Don't just pick on something because it has to be done to finish your promotion; actually give some thought to what a customer would appreciate and then offer that incentive. In fact, to generate even more interest, offer a Twixclusive and engage your followers to find out what they would like to have as an incentive. Make out a list and Tweet that – all those who complete the Flock to Unflock Campaign will be awarded with one of these incentives.

- Find out how many retweets you require. This is a promotional activity, so set your initial bar at the average amount of Retweets you'd normally get and then increase it, based on your followers' response.

- Create anticipation. This is the most important step of any promotional campaign, obviously! You'll have to be extra careful – you don't want to overdo it, but you must be able to create the air of suspense required to draw enough attention to your business. Tweet about the campaign launch, have countdown Tweets (maybe once a day), hashtag and trend as much as you can and do your best to increase excitement so that your audience responds and actually participates!

- Once the campaign is launched, make sure you stay on top of the game by constantly Tweeting promotion specifics. Be very precise and clear in what your audience must do to earn the incentive. Tweet to them countdowns and encourage them to complete the campaign to unlock their gift.

- Reward them finally. Once they have completed the required Retweets that you set, unflock their incentive. Link them to your website or Tweet it to them – make sure you take feedback from them about it!

As you can see, the Flock to Unflock Campaign is really just another contest in disguise, which is a nice segue into how you can host contests on Instagram and Twitter. The type of contest that you can hold itself varies from business to business, campaign to campaign. These are just extremely general guidelines I am telling you about; you can go ahead and customize or even invent new ideas to make sure your business gets the attention it deserves.

Contests on Twitter or Instagram are also known as Giveaways. They are an excellent marketing tool that will help you engage with your audience and find out what they are thinking; it will get you the visibility you need and it will endear you to your followers in a way that you will not be able to achieve otherwise.

Now what you to choose to give away as a contest prize is one of the most important decisions you will make. You want to make sure that customers return to you and keep following you on all social platforms; that means that you must impress them with your offers and remain true to your promises. Obviously, you are going to pick some part of your product as a prize; make sure that it is of good quality and will appeal to your customer while still being economically expendable on your budget. Word of mouth for small businesses is essential – you have to make sure that your contest winners are satisfied with what they get and will continue to advocate and follow you even after the contest is over. It's a good place to conduct clearance sales of old goods, but do not compromise on customer satisfaction, even when giving away freebies!

A good idea is to get a gift custom ordered for the sake of your contest alone, but this can be an expensive option. You will have to plan your budget and set aside the required amount for promotion accordingly. You could also get your contest winner to come to your store or view online products and pick out what they want for themselves within a budget limit or the pieces that you choose to put up as prizes. This is a brilliant way of engaging your audience – they feel so much more involved and special if they get such individual attention and they will definitely promote you even more. A free gift card with a specified amount they can spend on your goods is a good option too – just remember, this entire set is a costly bag of items, so make sure your budget can afford it!

Contest winner announcements are another landmine you will have to navigate. You want to make sure that they are not too ostentatious, so that the other customers do not feel cheated. At the same time, you do want to make a big deal out of your winner so that they return to your again. A good way of doing this is to follow up with your winner to make sure that they are enjoying the gifts they have won – take feedback from them as to if and where you are lacking in your product and then correct those areas. Such specific attention to them will make them feel part of your community and build brand loyalty. You could also post pictures of them using your product or get them to Tweet about their experience to further give you more visibility.

The last thing to consider before you jump into conducting contests on Twitter and Instagram is how often you will hold them. Obviously, they cannot be your only promotional strategy – they must augment your overall market plan that must include all social media platforms. So how many times in a year will you conduct it? Again, the answer will change with the nature, scope and type of business you run. My advice is to hold a trail run once – check out how much it costs, how much and what type of interest it generates in your customers, how much visibility you get in return, etc. weigh the pros and cons like always and then decide – usually, a minimum of 5-6 contests in a year is doable, though you will need to space them out properly.

And then, when you have considered all these- hold a contest! There are many, many types of contests you can hold – here are a few of them!

Contest #1 – Walk in to the Store Contest

Easy as this contest sounds, it is probably a bit more difficult to sell it to your customers since it involves legwork on their part. But if you can get it done right, it is a brilliant way of increasing visibility for both your online promotion as well as your actual, physical store! Contest rules are simple – Tweet about your campaign at the beginning and announce that you are holding your shop open for free trials on one afternoon.

The customers can walk in at any time and check out your products. You could offer them a free sample if you can afford it. Once they are in your store, ask them to take picture of themselves undergoing the free trial and then post it on Instagram or Twitter and get them to like and retweet. At the end of the contest, pick the person with the most likes or retweets as your winner.

Now, this kind of a contest is brilliant to direct traffic to your store, but it may not always go well with the type of product you are selling. For instance, if it is a small boutique selling high-end clothing, then this is an amazing idea – get your customers to post pictures of themselves wearing gorgeous new outfits! However, if you run something like an electronics store or a used bookstore, you may find it a bit more difficult to offer a free trial; free samples may be the way to go instead.

So as I have already mentioned previously, customize your contest to suit you and your product. Don't forget to set contest deadline validity, create a special hashtag for this purpose and take feedback from the winner about the product and their experience!

Contest #2 – Random Selection Contest

This is possibly the easiest method of conducting a contest on Twitter or Instagram. As the name suggests, you pick your winners at random. It is similar to the Flock to unflock campaign in that you get your followers to promote you – get them to like a post on Instagram or Retweet your tweet to a set number of times. Also remember to set a deadline within which they must hit the target; once the deadline passes, open your Twitter and Instagram and then at random, pick one of your followers to receive your prize. Make sure to announce that it is a random selection contest so that they don't feel cheated.

After the contest is over, do not forget to take feedback from them. Request them to post a picture of themselves with your product on Instagram or Tweet about their experience in the contest.

Contest #3 – Maximum Likes/Tweets Contest

Again, this is a pretty obvious type of contest to conduct; instead of picking your winner out at random, you pick the person who hits the maximum number of likes for you on Instagram or has the most number of Retweets on Twitter. You begin your campaign with an announcement of the contest and then Tweet or post the promotional ad/video/picture/message. Then announce that the person who likes your post the most or the person who manages to retweet your promotional message the most will win the contest. Again, this is a variant of the Flock to Unflock Campaign that you can modify to suit your needs.

Another way of conducting this contest is to get your customers to do the posting themselves, instead of you putting up that first Tweet. You start by creating a special hashtag for this particular contest and then Tweet or post about that. Announce that you are having your contest and then set a theme or a guideline that your customers must follow. Using that idea, ask them to post anything in relation – a picture of themselves using the product, a Tweet about the product's quality, etc., etc. Set a deadline for the end of the contest and monitor their posts regularly to make sure proper promotion takes place.

At the end of the contest, the Instagram account with the most number of likes for their post or picture, and the Twitter account that has the most number of Retweets of the customer's promotional message of you is the one that wins! The best idea is to ask them to post pictures of them using the product – people love to take selfies and post them online. So in a situation like this, it becomes a dual benefit; your customers enjoy the social media attention and you definitely get visibility!

Contest #4 – Video Contest

While Instagram and Twitter do not allow you to post videos as long as the ones on YouTube or even Facebook, a simple video contest maybe just what you need to get the visibility you are looking for! Instagram, at least, is meant for mobile photography – make full use of it. The premise of the contest is very simple. Just get your customers to post a video of themselves using your product and then add the contest hashtag to it. Keep the video short and simple – maybe to 10-15 seconds – and ask them to add a caption stating why they like or even dislike your product.

How you choose the winners is up to you. You could go for the person with the most number of likes or retweets for their video. Or you could choose a person at random. Or you could even announce that the person with the best caption or most creative video design will win. Make sure that they know what they are signing up for and be honest about it.

Again, this contest is a deal breaker for a lot of businesses, especially given the selfie craze of today's world. People love posting pictures and videos of themselves and given that they want to look good to their audience, they will be extra careful with their video. You get a wide visibility and you are able to build a loyal customer base!

Don't forget winner announcement, contest deadline, contest hashtag and winner follow up feedback.

Contest #5 – Website Contest

Unlike the other type of contests, this one is not exclusively limited to Twitter or Instagram. The challenge itself does not happen on either of these social platforms; they take place on your company website and you make use of these two to promote the contest that, in turn, promotes you and your business. It is a roundabout way of doing things, but marketing has never been easy! So your posts and Tweets will be geared towards spreading news – you will have post reminders, contest details and the like using the special hashtag you must make for this purpose.

Obviously, you cannot simply state the name, time and place – that's boring and is not going to capture any attention whatsoever. You want your customers to like and retweet your posts, so make sure you make them interesting, eye catchy, fun and engaging. Don't forget to provide a link to your website or the contest page in your captions and tweet reminder hashtags and countdown hashtags to get them interested!

Contest #6 – Shout-out Contest

Any regular user of social media will know – the best way to gain more publicity and followers is to give and get shout-outs from other users. This is, perhaps, a tad more popular on Instagram than on Twitter, but you can definitely use both to set up this kind of contest. Giving shout-outs is the easiest thing; all you have to do is to post a picture or put up a Tweet by tagging the other account and then given them a *'shout-out'*. You are, in essence, asking all those who are following you to go check out that account and if they like, then follow them too.

Again, you get your contest participants to do your promotion for you – get them to give your regular shout-outs. At the end of the contest, the person with the most number of shout-outs wins; monitor the traffic to your accounts to make sure that it has actually been effective as a promotional strategy, especially since giving a shout-out is not that hard an activity.

Don't forget your contest deadline, contest hashtag or winner feedback!

These are some of the most basic contest types you can conduct on Instagram and Twitter to gain visibility. As I said, they are not rigid rules you need to follow; every business is different, so customize your contest to suit your overall marketing strategy. Holding regular contests works for small businesses because you get the opportunity to engage your audience and get personal with them. Everyone loves a little something free and when you offer them that, you capture their attention and gain visibility.

Remember, every time someone tags you or gives you a shout-out, their entire fan following gets to know about you. If some of these people follow you and they start tagging you, their followers start taking note of you too – it's the best type of cyclical promotion and you must work hard to achieve it.

Now that you know the different kinds of contests that you can host, here are a few more things you should consider when you conduct them –

- Why are you holding the contest, other than the obvious promotional reason? A contest that is absolutely random and has no particular theme or goal is rather boring; keep to a central idea and then use that as your hashtag to make sure your customers remain interested!
- Only if your contest goal is defined will you be able to make your tweets and posts specific and interesting! This way, you will be able to pick out

who your target customers are and then edit your pictures and tweets and tags according to that.

- Without the purpose of your contest, you really cannot come up with a suitable prize for the winner. We have already talked about what you can give away and what you can afford to spend on – who your target audience is and what the purpose of hosting the contest is will help you decide what to give out as a reward.

- Make sure to get visibility for your contest by posting regularly about it! Don't forget to create a contest hashtag and make sure you remind your participants about using it as much as possible so that it becomes a trending topic. Also remember – too many posts and tweets annoy, too less make you forgettable. Ideally, one post a day is a good choice; it will remind the audience that something exciting is happening while not being too irritating by constantly popping up on their feed.

- Contest hashtags are the most important thing in a Twitter or Instagram contest. Without it, you are in big trouble – how will you keep track of every single customer's posting? Remind your contestants that they must use it or they will not be considered; it will help you manage the entries much better. Also, when you make the hashtag, remember – it cannot be something that is too commonly used, or anyone who is tagging with it will be considered automatically, even if they are not taking part in your contest! The tag should be specific to you and your contest, so keep it simple but creative.

- A good idea is to make it compulsory to Follow your account on either (or both) Instagram or Twitter if they want to take part in the contest. This brings in more visibility for you, though there isn't much to stop them from Unfollowing you once the contest is over. It's up to you to keep them from doing that!

- Keep an eye on the contest deadline; too small a time frame and you will not get enough participants. Too big a time window and the contest will be forgotten altogether. Generally, regular contests that last for around two or three weeks is a good idea; having regular Twitter countdowns really gets them moving, since the human psyche is wired to panic at deadlines! A bigger prize, which involves a lot of expenditure on your part, may require a bigger time frame – have a longer contest in this case, given that the prize is not small. This builds brand loyalty, but can be expensive and time consuming, so be sure you are willing to afford that.

- Don't forget to promote your contest on every single social media platform you are active on! Even if the contest is only on Twitter and/or Instagram, promotion must happen across all your accounts, whether Facebook, Pinterest or YouTube or even your own blog! Provide links to the contest in all pages and make sure your customers are following you on all platforms.

- Make sure you know how you are going to deliver the prize to your winners. Are they located close enough to geographically that you can give it to them in person? Do you have to have it shipped to their home? In the latter case, how much money will you have to spend to do so? Is it worth that cost and can you afford that? Take a look at these options before you pick someone to be your winner.

As is obvious, hosting a contest is no easy job – it requires time, patience and careful strategizing. But if you can do it right, it will be an effective tool in getting you visibility, building up a loyal customer base, attracting new and returning customers and overall increase traffic to your venture. A few quick things you should keep in mind when you post or tweet something –

- Do not limit your posts and tweets to product details or campaign details alone. If you leave your accounts looking like a catalogue of your business, it's going to bore anybody who comes to view your page. Instead, make your posts fun and engaging – talk to your customers to build a loyal base.
- Post about your business processes and give your followers a behind-the-scenes tour. It will make them feel special and connected to you to know how you make for them the product they use – it builds brand loyalty when they know how much hard work you put into making the best for them.
- Tweet about your employees and their lives and get them to LiveTweet and Q&A sessions. What you'll do in this case is foster a sense of community within your customer base; small businesses, more often than not, tend to be a poster child for this type of marketing. Make full use of it; get your workers to take part and they will also work harder at the

vindication of their work. And your customers' feel further connected to you and your business. Tweet your team building experiences, post pictures of lunches together and retweet your employees' tweets.

- Use the video option to post small advertisements. The advantage of Instagram or Twitter is that you don't pay millions to shoot small ads for a few seconds – all you need is a good quality camera, a few employees or friends to act out a 10 second script and some quality editing software that you can get for free from the internet. Obviously, given that you cannot post a long video on these platforms, you have no choice but to keep it short – make it catchy, make it fun and colorful. Add your tagline or jingle and make sure it represents you and your business. You yourself could act in it if you like, or you could get your employees to do it! Load it on to the computer, work a little editing magic and then post it. Share it, retweet it, like it and spread it around – you don't need much investment in advertisements this way!

- Make full and proper use of the hashtag facility on both Instagram and Twitter. Even if you are not hosting contests, tag your posts. Tags are how people search for and come across accounts – you should tag not just your brand name and product but also related ideas so that people can stumble across you when they are looking for something. For instance, if you are a boutique owner and selling non-standard sized clothing for both people of extremely small and extremely large stature, you should tag things like *#bodypositivty* or *#beautybeyondsize* or even *#everysizeisoursize*. Think about it and pick those tags that people are likely to use. Also remember, the more the people use your tag, the more popular it becomes and you can become a trending topic, which automatically gains more visibility for you!

- Engage your audience. Give regular shout-outs to regular customers and like and comment on their posts so that they know you value their opinion. Make them feel special – do not forget to take their feedback! Post and tweet information and pictures once you have incorporated their feedback; it makes them feel even more special that you are actually taking into consideration whatever they are saying and it goes a long way in building a sense of loyalty. And as you build your business profile and become popular, your shout-out will bring them visibility, making it a mutually symbiotic relationship!

- Connect with other businesses on Instagram and Twitter and see if the two of you can't work together to promote both your businesses. Two similar businesses could really work this out. For instance, if you are a boutique owner, get a fashion designer with her own clothing line to represent you! You could promote their next show in return for a small ad with him or her in it. Give and get shout-outs, create user friendly tags and promote one another – use the power of social media to its fullest!

Remember, ultimately, Twitter and Instagram (and every other social media platform, for that matter) are for those who are active online. You cannot simply post once a month and vanish for days together; to get and maintain visibility, you must constantly post and tweet – you need to engage your audience and keep them interested if you want traffic to your accounts, and in turn, business, to increase.

Chapter 9: Identifying Your Customers

There can be many types of customers and it is important for a company to identify the different ones to connect with them better and be able to sell more to each. In this chapter, we will look at the distinct category of people that you need to know about.

80-90% customers

This is the first category of customers and mostly your best category as well. people that belong to tis category are well equipped with the knowledge of what they are looking to buy. They are not going to waste any time and go straight to what they want. So, to market to such people, you have to present to them a well organized website or social media site that will allow them to pick what they want as the very first thing. You can then give them practical suggestions that will go well with what they have already bought. For example, you can offer them a coffee maker when they buy a toaster. These people will be welcoming of good and practical ideas and you must put in the appropriate efforts to please them. But remember to keep it sensible and don't take their intelligence for granted. These types are also most likely going to be your return customers. They might not walk in as often but will surely keep coming back to you. you have to put in all possible efforts to hold on to them.

60 -70% customers

The next category of customers is the 60-70%. These customers can be just as smart as the people from the previous category, but, will not be as organized as them. they will not have a pre-prepared list of what they wish to buy from you. They will walk in and hope to find something that they want to buy. You have to set up a website that will help them connect things and buy them. they should be in a particular sequence that will help them move from one category to the next. These people can get emotionally attached to certain brands and their products and choose to only buy the same ones over and over again. so, you have to try and create a place for your brand in their hearts, so that you can repeatedly get them to buy from you. these types can also be a little hard to convince and so, you have to put in appropriate efforts to convince them.

40- 50% customers

The 40-50% customers are those that are generally restless and fidgety. They are extremely disorganized and will have absolutely no agenda while shopping. They will mostly look at everything that is on offer and then pick something that they think is nice. These people are usually attracted to anything bright and fun. So, you have to put on offer everything that is fun and bright. It is a good trick to place it at the very end of the store so that they are forced to pick it up. Online, you can offer it at the check out page where they will not be able to refuse it. since these customers are extremely impatient, you have to make the check out process easy for them. They should find it easy to navigate through the pages and also check out easily. You can keep directing them to the final page to help keep their interest.

20 – 30% customers

The next category is the 20-30% customers. These can be hard to convince and will come around only once a month to do all the buying at once. They can be tough to deal with, especially if they have come in groups. The best way to deal with them is to offer them something they cannot refuse. For example, offer them something that they can carry for their loved ones as this category will be highly interested in buying something for their loved ones. You can offer them a buy one get one, which will make them happy. These people are also easy to retain, provided you give them the best offers.

0% customers

This is the last category of people and as you can guess, they are extremely hard to please. In fact, they will not even be interested in listening to what you have to say to them. Even if you tried your best to tell them something, they will only be bothered about what they want to buy and have nothing to do with your suggestions. It is best to ignore such customers and let them shop by themselves.

These form the different types of customers that you have to be on the lookout for.

The 80/20 analysis

It is a good idea for you to take up the 80/20 analysis. The 80/20 analysis is one where you do statistical calculations to find the best product, social media site or customer group that is bringing in the most business.

The theory states that 20% of something will bring in 80% of your business. So, you can find the 20% by doing a few simple calculations. Start by deciding on what you wish to calculate the percentages for. Once you decide, write down the names of the different options. For example, if you are looking for the best social media site then write down names of all of them one below the other. In the next column, write down the number of people that are following you through each site. Next, total everything cumulatively. Now divide the initial number by the cumulative total to find the best site. Similarly, do the calculations for the others to find the best one. But remember that the total need not always come up to 100%. Don't mix the 20% and 80% together.

Conclusion

In today's technological world, no business can survive if it does not keep up with the fast paced advancements that science offers us. You must be willing to keep yourself up to date with the changing market trends; the consumer is more informed and more demanding than before, and you need to be on your toes to cater to their every need, lest you lose your business.

Internet marketing and e-commerce is the way to go these days! At the click of a mouse or a few taps of a keyboard, you have access to a global market that is quite demanding and powerful; you will have to work hard to keep up with them, but your business will expand like never before! Use the golden marketing nuggets I have told you – they will get you started in the world of online marketing and business running! Remember – these are just the guidelines to make your beginning; you have to keep creating and innovating on your own so that your business doesn't become stagnant and run into loss.

The market is a fickle place, whether virtual or real. Play it expertly with a keen eye and it will reward beyond your imagination. Listen to your customers, take their feedback and keep on improving – these are the best tips you can follow to an effective marketing strategy!

Thank you for choosing this book. I hope you found it informative!

Bonus

Thanks for making it this far in your education. If you want the real multiplier effect and to take your business skills to the next level, I recommend the easy-to-follow quick tips below. Whether you are running a company or just trying to free up some time so you can spend more time doing the things you love, get more done this week or your money back ;) (it's free!).

Visit https://funnelb.leadpages.co/smarter-not-harder-business/

Top 10 Productivity Tips & Hacks GUARANTEED to Unlock Massive Amounts of Time, Crush Decision Fatigue, and Skyrocket Your Efficiency and Effectiveness

For physical copy, enter in URL: https://funnelb.leadpages.co/smarter-not-harder-business/

Recommended Reading

Complete Your Business Relationship Skills Education With a Click Away:

Management: Golden Nugget Methods to Manage Effectively - Teams, Personnel Management, Management Skills, and Conflict Resolution

Communication: Golden Nugget Methods to Communicate Effectively - Interpersonal, Influence, Social Skills, Listening

Take Your Business Skills Further for Financial Freedom or Corporate Dominance:

Small Business: EXACT BLUEPRINT on How to Start a Business - Home Business, Entrepreneur, and Small Business Marketing

Sales: Foolproof Method to CRUSH Your Numbers - Selling, Sales Techniques, and Sales Strategy